Marcus Katz & Tali Goodwin

Cover: 'The Sun', Tyldwick Tarot © by Neil Lovell

http://www.malpertuis.co.uk/tyldwick/

KDP Edition

Published by Forge Press (2020)

1 Wood Cottage, Old Windebrowe, Keswick, Cumbria CA12 4NT

Find us in discussion with more than 35,000 Tarot Students, Readers and Teachers for the best in innovative Tarot in our Facebook group **Tarot Professionals** and enjoy the membership benefits of the Tarot Association at **www.tarotassociation.net**.

Tarosophy® is a registered trademark.

Preface

Before you begin, you may wish to join thousands of other tarot students, readers, authors, artists, and enthusiasts in our free Facebook group **Tarot Professionals** if you have any questions about Tarot, and also download our free 22-page keyword guide to tarot cards and 12 standard spreads from our site:

www.mytarotcardmeanings.com

Introduction

In this second Kickstart book of exclusive and innovative Tarosophy teaching, you will take your knowledge from the first keywords and concepts of Tarot in *Flip* and now *Twist* them into whole new ways of reading and engaging with Tarot!

This book is also a standalone title in that it encourages you to play with Tarot methods and spreads until you become confident to create your own in response to the question being presented to you. This is one of the hallmarks of an excellent reader and a skill we encourage our intermediate Tarot students to develop.

We have had a lot of creative fun in bringing you this book, which draws on three decades of Tarot practice and teaching experience. We look forwards to seeing you on the journey ahead!

Marcus Katz, The Tarosophist

& Tali Goodwin, TaliTarot

The Layout of this Kickstart Book

This book provides a compendium of original ideas in Tarot. We have provided a subtitle for each method presented in this book to indicate **one** possible usage of the spread or application. These are not to be taken as anything other than a general guideline, as the whole purpose of *Twist* is to demonstrate how anything may be *twisted* into service of divination through the Tarot. However, some of these methods have been used over many years and have demonstrated their power in specific circumstances which are given here as a good starting-point.

The methods range from standard spreads for beginners to more intermediate and advanced methods best suited for experienced readers. We have not indicated which level we believe a method to be best suited to encourage your exploration of as many methods as possible.

Some of these methods are for self-discovery work and others are straightforward divination and prediction. A few of the methods given here begin to demonstrate how Tarot may be used as a proactive key back into the Universe to effect change though their magick. That particular approach is explored further in our following KickStart book, *Tarot Inspire*.

For selected methods and approaches we have given further reading suggestions to deepen your appreciation of the inspiration for the methods. You can also develop that method or approach further by referring to the source material and designing your own *spread variations.*

Who knows, you may even come to have a spread or method named after you, and then a variant, such as the **McCord Variant (Marcia's Loop) of Rachel's Game.**[1]

---

[1] This is a variant way of seeing the Fool's Journey suggested by reader Marcia McCord during the Tarot Town Halloween Ball, 2010. We were playing Rachel's Game, which is another way of seeing the intrinsic journey each of the Major cards implies.

A Brief note on Attunement

In Tarosophy we consider a decks *attunement* to a reading or divinatory question. We choose particular decks for specific readings or methods. That is not to say a gifted reader cannot attune a deck outside its normal range – We have seen profound spiritual readings performed with the **Hello** (Kitty) **Tarot** deck and patently ridiculous questions answered with good humor by the **Thoth Tarot** of Aleister Crowley and Frieda Harris.

In *Tarot Twist* we provide some ideas for which decks might be attuned to some of the methods given here, for example, a method involving layers is best performed with Emily Carding's **Transparent Tarot** or **Transparent Oracle**. A method involving outdoor work is best performed with an appropriate pagan deck whose symbols reflect the environment, such as **Twilight Realm** deck by Beth Wilder – very appropriate if outdoors at night by candle-light.

We deal with issues of attunement and the power of performing deliberately *discordant* readings in *Tarosophy*. In this present guide, we will give some ideas for attuned decks where appropriate for specific methods, such as the Negative Confessions method and spread.

The Tarot Twist

Whilst many books speak of the Fool's Journey through the Major Arcana of the Tarot, which is inevitably a form of the archetypal Hero's Journey observed by Campbell, in Tarot Twist we see how each card *twists* into its successor. This perspective can assist you see the Majors through a novel perspective, allowing for powerful one-card readings, or new ways of seeing these cards when they appear in a reading.

The Tarot Twist with Majors can be demonstrated by seeing aspects of the Fool card, reversed. These include logic instead of chaos, control instead of freedom, and guile instead of innocence. At a deeper level, we also see in the Fool reversed a *twist* of the essential silence of the Fool into the spoken word, the Logos. All these twisted meanings are of course embodied by the upright Magician, the first card in the sequence of the Majors. They also accord with the attributes of Mercury, corresponding to this card.

So, if we *twist* the Fool, he mutates into the Magician. This rule holds true throughout the entire sequence of the Majors. The Magician, with his "show and tell" on the table, *twists* into the High Priestess, who hides her secrets behind the veil; the virgin High Priestess then *twists* into the pregnant Empress ... this might also be termed the Tarot Topple, as one card falls inevitably into the next when taken to its extreme.

Firstly, we will play Tarot Twist with the Majors in our own way, and then we would encourage you to sit for a while and perhaps consider your own twists between two cards in sequence, for example how might the Wheel twist into Justice? Imagine the Wheel turning; consider perhaps the meanings of fate and karma. Take these to their logical extension, blow them out of proportion, and twist them as if you were twisting the card, morphing it into the next card, Justice. What do you feel or see happening – what tensions exist between the cards, where do they neatly overlap?

While doing this exercise, you may experience deeper meanings of the individual cards as your unconscious processes are forced into deep comparative activity – a sort of brain-training for your intuition, like a spiritual Sudoku.

So, you might feel the Wheel spinning, then consider the axle, then look at Justice and see how still that card image looks (on the RWS deck) and feel the pull between constant motion and absolute stillness and balance.

You might be thinking of the axle and scales, how they both balance forces. In doing this, you might begin to feel the *twist* as the Wheel Twists into Justice, expressed as "Regularity twists into Law". You might even suddenly get the idea that "habit twists into a rule" or other similar expressions. You now have a new meaning and insight into the Wheel, as "habit", if you did not already consider the Wheel to represent that concept.

So here are our Tarot Twists, for your initial consideration and as an example of the game in play.

Illus. The Snake That Twists.

… twists everything into nothing …

0 : FOOL

Twists innocence into guile

I : MAGICIAN

Twists communication into concealment

II : PRIESTESS

Twists seeding into fertility

III : EMPRESS

Twists nature into nurture

IV : EMPORER

Twists power into control

V : HIEROPHANT

Twists regulation into choice

VI : LOVERS

Twists contentment into drive

VII : CHARIOT

Twists rhythm into rhyme

VIII : STRENGTH

Twists relationship into self-awareness

IX : HERMIT

Twists the journeyer into the journey

X : WHEEL

Twists the revolution into the law

XI : JUSTICE

Twists peace into stillness

XII : HANGED MAN

Twists sacrifice into reward

XIII : DEATH

Twists renewal into change

XIV : TEMPERANCE

Twists connection into attachment

XV : DEVIL

Twists contraction into explosion

XVI : TOWER

Twists confusion into vision

XVII : STAR

Twists light into reflection

XVIII : MOON

Twists identity into awareness

XIX : SUN

Twists fuel into creation

XX : LAST JUDGEMENT

Twists noise into signal

XXI : UNIVERSE

Twists everything into nothing

0: FOOL

… Twists nothing into everything …

Illus. The Snake That Twists Again.

You will see that we have created this Twist as a loop, which indicates how the twists return back around the cycle in an endless sequence. The Majors are a **revolutionary** process, through which the Fool tumbles, turns and twists in an endless and timeless journey – perhaps because the Fool is an image of that endless and timeless journey.

You might also consider placing the Major cards on a Möbius Strip, with the twist being where the Fool and the Universe coincide. If you follow that route, you might develop an Escher-type Tarot deck, which would be fascinating but somewhat difficult to shuffle!

The keywords one can derive for the cards are the first word which applies to the preceding card, and the second word which applies to the following card. This means that each card has two keywords, one from the twist before, one going into the twist following. Thus, the Sun is both Awareness **and** Fuel. The Hanged Man is Stillness **and** Sacrifice, the Death card is reward **and** renewal.

This builds further from our simple keywords in *Tarot Flip* and gives a slightly different perspective. Now you can also see how a card can mutate its meaning based on the cards before and after it — or around it — in a reading.

Using the Twists in a Reading

To perform a Twist Tarot reading, simply take the Majors out of your deck. Shuffling these twenty-two cards, ask your question and select one card. Lay that card on the table and read the appropriate twist phrase.

For example, my question is "How will I get the most from my visit to a client tonight. Will it be a successful visit?"

I draw THE STAR.

The twist for this is "light into reflection". This suggests that I should take whatever light (information) is given to me in the session and twist it into self-reflection. I may learn more about myself than my client.

You can further follow the twist strip by then simply following the next twists, so we can then see with the next twist, THE MOON, I should see from that reflection of the upcoming visit an opportunity to define myself more fully and become aware more of my own abilities and skills.

The Twist will work for all questions and turn a one-card reading into a powerful sequence of interpretation. It can also work well for analyzing previous events where the learning outcome is unclear.

Tarot Timings

Whilst you practiced your first readings using *Tarot Flip*, you may have already encountered a common question asked of readers, which is simply "When?" So, whilst the reading may have predicted success in employment, travel, a move, a relationship (or not), the Querent will equally be interested in the timing of the events or changes.

Tarot is not an exact science. It is a divinatory art of interpretation. If we could all make an exact mapping system of the Universe, accurate to the exact moment and event in all its detail, we would create this Universe!

> *On Exactitude in Science* . . . In that Empire, the Art of Cartography attained such Perfection that the map of a single Province occupied the entirety of a City, and the map of the Empire, the entirety of a Province. In time, those Unconscionable Maps no longer satisfied, and the Cartographers Guilds struck a Map of the Empire whose size was that of the Empire, and which coincided point for point with it. The following Generations, who were not so fond of the Study of Cartography as their Forebears had been, saw that that vast Map was Useless, and not without some Pitilessness was it, that they delivered it up to the Inclemencies of Sun and Winters. In the Deserts of the West, still today, there are Tattered Ruins of that Map, inhabited by Animals and Beggars; in all the Land there is no other Relic of the Disciplines of Geography.
>
> Suarez Miranda,Viajes de varones prudentes, Libro IV,Cap. XLV, Lerida, 1658 [This is a literary fiction concocted by Borges – Marcus]
>
> From Jorge Luis Borges, *Collected Fictions*, Translated by Andrew Hurley (Penguin, 1999)

Equally, as we see in Borges above, a 1:1 mapping system is too close to the arising manifestation of life to work in this way. If you wanted to remove the "interpretative lag" between your Tarot deck and a Horse Race for example, you would simply create a small deck of cards with the names of the horses on them, and shuffle the deck and every time you stopped and laid the cards out, they would appear in the order for which the horses would finish the race. It is obvious the Universe does not work like that on this level!

So, the cards are "close enough" to give us connected and relevant answers irrespective of time and space, but not so close that they are identical to the events. In between is where our divinatory art is practiced.

Whilst admitting that, let us look at two methods for giving predictive timings, one interpretative, and the other direct.

Method One: Timing Interpretative

Using a standard spread such as the Celtic Cross, we can analyze the cards for a general feeling of the timing of an event. This is because we accept that the cards themselves correspond to a deeper structure, equally modeled by Kabbalah, where the Universe is an *emanation*.

As such, it flows through the images and numbers, one to ten, in a cosmic unfolding. Our spread should reflect the stage in this process which is present at the time of the reading.

Equally, the cards in any "future" and "Outcome" positions will reflect this timing. As will the cards in the "past" or "previous" positions.

So if we take a look firstly at the overall spread, simply ignore the Majors (which are placeholders of the timeless and archetypal forces) and the Court Cards (which indicate the levels of energy at play) and look at the Minor cards in the spread.

Firstly, take an average of the numbers. That indicates the overall stage on a 1-10 manifestation. If you have 5 Minor cards in your Celtic Cross, and they are the Ace (1) of Wands, 3 of Pentacles, 7 of Swords, 5 of Cups and 9 of Cups that equates to $1+3+7+5+9 = 25$. Divide that by the 5 cards to get the average and we get $25/5 = 5$. This is an exact half-way between 1-10. It shows the situation at present is only half-way to its manifestation.

We can further analyze the reading by then looking at the Outcome card (which might indicate a rapid resolution, say the Blasted Tower) and see that whilst the situation is only half-way manifest, it is rapidly approaching a climax, meaning a sudden acceleration!

When you have an average, you can apply it to the overall timescale likely by saying, the situation is likely to be anything between 1 month – 1 year as you told me. I see it being manifest by 6 months (half-way).

Method Two: Timing Direct

Take the following six *Timing Significators* out of the Majors:

- Blasted Tower
- Death
- Moon
- Sun
- High Priestess
- Empress

The Wheel is taken out and placed face-up in the center of the table. This signifies the wheel of Karma, cause-and-effect, the changes of life and Time itself. It corresponds to the Hebrew letter *Kaph*, meaning "palm of hand" and it is the universal hand in which all fate and destiny is written.

Get a clock or watch and shuffle the six timing significators for exactly 60 seconds. This represents the passage of time and incorporates it into the method to replicate the notion of time.

Lay out the six cards about the Wheel in a clock face. Here it **is** important which order and location we place the cards, so it is indicated below.

Illus. Timing Wheel Spread.

Now ask the Querent (or yourself) whether you would wish the event predicted to transpire immediately (1), very soon (2), soon (3), in the near future (4), later (5) or never (6). Take the card in that position and read it as in the following table.

Timing Significator	Interpretation
Blasted Tower	Immediately, very soon
Death	Later rather than sooner
Moon	1 month/soon
Sun	1 year/later
High Priestess	Who knows? In its own time.
Empress	9 months

Again, we must recall that timing is not an accurate science and it may well be that you gain the cross-services of an Astrologer for such predictive timing or acquire astrological skills yourself.[2]

---

[2] We recommend the works and services of Lyn Birkbeck: www.lynbirkbeck.com. His *Instant Astrologer* book is a classic (also published as the *Watkins Astrological Handbook*), and the software that accompanies it is invaluable.

78 Methods and Spreads for Tarot Twists

In the following section of *Tarot Twist*, we present the new methods and spreads making up the 78 innovations of *Twist*. These have been created over many years to demonstrate how Tarot may be taken as a basic alphabet (cards) and grammar (correspondences) and turned into a complete language of divination in direct dialogue with the Universe.

Whilst some of these ideas and exercises are basic positional spreads, others are magical or mystical exercises of spiritual import. In Tarosophy we see the Tarot as a primary illustration of the Western Esoteric Initiatory System (WEIS) and whilst you need not subscribe to this view nor recognize it for use of these methods, we would encourage you to approach some of these exercises with appropriate consideration.

We introduce in this *Twist* many new concepts that have been used by Marcus for some three decades, in over ten thousand personal readings, face-to-face with Querents. These include *pulled* spreads, *fractal* spreads, *split*-spreads, *branching* spreads, *Gated* spreads, and other types of spread which have many further variations. The *Tarosophy* book has others, including *tumbler* spreads, and *linked* and *chained* spreads.

We will discover in these pages the mysteries of Pooh Bear's profound questions, next to the dark *grimoire* of the Typhonian Book of the Spider. We will range from shamanic practice to the Hermetic order of the Golden Dawn. We will riff on Edgar Allan Poe and Ancient Egyptian burial practice. We will even face Death itself and dream Tarot. You will take your Tarot for a walk, push it off tables, set fire to it, lose it to the wind and generally play fast and loose with the deck.

This is a steam-train of a book to encourage you to adopt a playful, curious and creative attitude to your Tarot. There are no hard and fast rules, just you, the deck, and the Universe.

Have fun and hold on tight – here we go!

The Settler, Warrior, Nomad Spread

Using the Power of three Tribes to divine how to deal with a tricky situation.

In this opening spread of *Tarot Twist*, we present a relatively straightforward spread. However, of course, we add a twist to it. This is what in Tarosophy is called a **split spread**. That is to say, we split certain parts of the full deck out to do the reading. Sometimes we use parts of the deck in different areas of the reading, sometimes we just use one part of the deck for the whole reading.

In this case we use only the **Minors** (Ace to Ten of all four Suits). This is because we only want to look at the down-and-dirty real-world events and advice for a tricky situation – not confused with archetypal and abstract forces (of the Majors) or the perspective of other forces or people (the Courts). So just take out all 40 Minor cards and deal them as you wish into this pattern whilst considering your question/situation – or the question/situation of your Querent.

Another Twist we apply to this straightforward 6-card spread is that we can also use numerology (from a Kabbalistic background) in a very simple manner to discover in the reading which of the three approaches being examined will lead to the fastest result, and which one will take longest to bring resolution. This allows a basic consideration of predictive timing to be taken into account.

It might be, for example, that the better of two options of three (where one is negative) is actually shown taking a longer time. So, the Querent who wants a faster resolution might follow the advice of the lesser of the positive results because that one comes out faster.

You will also note that in all examples we rarely use numbers to indicate positions as these tend to train students in reading the cards in a linear sequence, 1,2,3… whereas experienced readers will cast their gaze over the whole reading first and then read it as they find it. So long as you determine the order of laying out the spread first or by your own choice in the moment, that is the important thing.

This spread is inspired by the book *Warriors, Settlers, Nomads* by Terence Watts. You can also take a short questionnaire in the book (p. 14) to determine your particular tribal makeup!

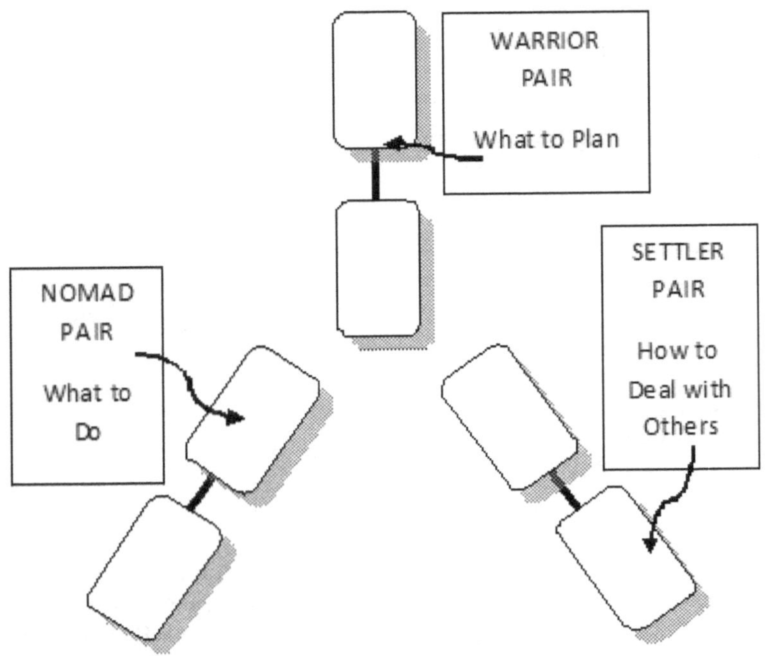

Illus. Settler, Warrior, Nomad Spread.

Having laid out the six cards you can read them as three different aspects of what a "Warrior" would advise (planning, strategy), what a "Nomad" would advise (acting, movement) and what a "Settler" would advise (getting on with others, taking account of the environment). Each of these three aspects may agree with each other or shed different aspects on the same overall response.

Use *Tarot Flip* to read the cards as pairs if you require further insight.

Where they all disagree, you can interpret the relative time-scale of each course of action by simply adding up the numbers of the two cards in each pair. The highest total is the one closest to happening. So if the two Nomad cards are a Four and a Three (totaling seven) and the Settler cards are an Ace and an Eight (totaling nine) and the Warrior pair is a Five and a Nine (totaling fourteen) it is the Warrior planning that will actually get the fastest and most immediate result.

This works on the basis that in Kabbalah, the world of action is the "10" of a sequence starting at "1" so numbers closer to 10 are closer to manifestation.

The What to Do Spread (Next Step Method)

An innovative method answering the question following a reading, "So what do I do?"

This is a practice which answers the usual client question after a first reading, which is "so what do I do about it?" or "what next?" This next step method can be done in two ways, as a divination or as a counseling/coaching tool, dependent on your own skills. This is one example of what Tarosophists call a progressive spread, one where the progression of the cards in sequence is taken as meaningful.

1. Perform a three-card reading for a simple question.

2. Lay the three cards out and then underneath each card select the "next" card in the sequence of the Minors, the next card "up the court" if a Court Card, or the next in sequence if a Major. For example, if the first card in your 3-card spread is the 8 of Wands, the card you put underneath it should be the 9 of Wands. If the card is the Ace of Cups, the card you put underneath it is the 2 of Cups. If the card is the Page of Pentacles, the "next" card is the Knight of Pentacles. If the Blasted Tower (XVI) then the Star (XVII).

If the card is at the "end" of the sequence, cycle round to the "start"; i.e. Ten of Wands becomes Ace of Wands, King of Swords becomes Page of Swords, the Universe/World become the Magician. The only card that has no "next" card is the Fool, of course! The Fool remains the Fool!

So, for example, we shuffle, split and deal a 3-card spread which is:

| Two of Wands | Knight of Pentacles | Hermit |

The cards we place underneath are therefore:

| Three of Wands | Queen of Pentacles | Wheel of Fortune |

Then look down each pair and ask, "how does this card become this next card?" Look for clues, for what must have happened "inbetween" the two cards. What did the Hermit do to become the Wheel of Fortune … perhaps give up his mountain retreat to go gambling?! How did the Knight become the Queen – other than the gender change, perhaps by gaining maturity through travelling the world?

Then take these three "bridging strategies" and put them together to create a narrative with a single theme, perhaps one of "maturity though experience", "trusting instinct", "Learning from others" or "going it alone".

This narrative will provide the "next step" required by the Querent to move out of their presently stuck situation. This is a powerful method and in dialogue with the Querent often provides innovative insight and coaching or counseling potential.

As a straight method of divination, simply perform your regular reading (say 3 or 5 cards) and lay out the "next step" cards below as described, leaving a gap between the cards. Then lay out cards from the deck 'between' the gaps which you may read as the 'step' the client is advised to take next to get onwards.

If a card which is the next step from another has already appeared in the reading (and therefore cannot be laid out) what might this signify?

This method, whilst being used and taught by Marcus for many years, was first presented at a UK Tarot workgroup in 2005 and is published in the *Tarot Shuffle* (issue 2), given out to Tarosophy Tarot Houses worldwide.

If you are interested in establishing a Tarosophy Tarot House, with 3-4 friends or fellow Tarot students, meeting on a monthly basis to develop your Tarot in these innovative methods, please contact us.

The Time Capsule Method

A Quantum Mechanics Method (also called Schrödinger's Spread)

For this method you will need a spare deck, perhaps one of those small mini-decks or novelty decks. You are about to set fire to it! Well, some of it at least!

This is for a question where you are totally unsure as to how something is going to pan out, fall into place, or resolve itself. It uses a strange phenomenon called the "observer effect". Whilst this is only apparent at the minute levels of the Universe studied by quantum physics, here we use it as a metaphor or model at a large Tarot-scale.

You will also need a small degree of patience and will-power in this method.

Take your deck and shuffle, considering the question or situation. Take out one card, face-down. Place it in a sealed bag or box and go bury it somewhere where you have easy access - and do not forget where it is buried! Leave the rest of the deck face-down.

Now leave the buried card and the face-down deck for about one week, during which time you may begin to wonder what the answer to your question is – which card is it out of 78 which is buried? Those of a pagan perspective may perform this between a New Moon and a Full Moon.

When you have built up your impatience to sufficient degree, go out and take your deck (minus the one buried card) to where that card is buried. Set light to the deck above the burial place of the one card.

At that present moment, it is impossible to tell if the card buried is any one particular card. It could well be that the Universe itself is in many states, with each of 78 different cards buried – or none, or something else entirely different.

It is only now at the moment that you dig the card up and look at it that the Universe sets itself – from your perspective – into the Universe in which that is the card that is in front of you. You may wish to keep this card or heed its advice and then burn it as with the rest of the deck.

Climb Inside Your Spread!

How to really get inside the spread and discover more than you first saw.

This method works well with a medium spread of 8-15 cards in any particular pattern. It is designed to get you looking at the cards in a different way. You can perform this method and then return to your original spread within a week and you will discover new insight.

1. Take the names of the cards in your spread.

2. Take a pad of "post-it" notes, or several small colored pads.

3. Write down one card from your reading on a separate note.

4. Go round your house (or room) and place the post-it notes in positions relative to your original spread.

5. Live inside the spread for several days to a week at most.

Notice when you notice the notes, look around from one note and see which others are closest and which ones you cannot see.

Watch which ones fall off from where you first placed them, or family members move them around, or write things on them.

Insight may come during the exercise, or when you then return to lay out the cards in the original spread.

The Negative Confessions Spread

A Test and Purification of your Soul through Tarot.

The Ancient Egyptian afterlife held within it a sacred journey of the soul, whose purpose was tested to ensure the deceased had lived a life according to *Ma'at*, the cosmic order or essential measure of truth. In this method we test ourselves according to a contemporary "declaration of innocence" in a ritual version of the so-called *negative confessions*.

The deck most *attuned* to this method is the **Thoth Tarot** by Aleister Crowley and Frieda Harris, or any other deck based on the Ancient Egyptian motif and symbols.

For each of the lines (some amended by this author, you may wish to modify them to your own code of conduct) we produce a Tarot *confessional card* to reflect the action we must take to pass that pylon. Take your deck, shuffle, reviewing your life thus far, and draw out the cards in sequence. You may wish to read aloud the confessions.

Between each of the 42 statements below, draw a card which will indicate the response of that particular gate, and whether you need to take action to pass that gate in the afterlife (or the here-and-now) and measure up to Ma'at. If for example you received the 9 of Cups against the second pylon, "I have not robbed with violence" you are probably clear at that gate.

> 1.   Hail, Long-Strider who comes from Heliopolis, I have not done iniquity.
>
> 2.   Hail, Embraced-by Fire who comes from Kher-aha, I have not robbed with violence.
>
> 3.   Hail, Divine-Nose who comes from Khemmenu, I have not done violence to another man.
>
> 4.   Hail, Shade-Eater who comes from the caverns which produce the Nile, I have not committed theft.
>
> 5.   Hail, Neha-hau who comes from Re-stau, I have not killed man or woman.
>
> 6.   Hail, double Lion God who comes from heaven, I have not lightened the bushel.

7.   Hail, Flint-Eyes who comes from Sekhem, I have not acted deceitfully.

8.   Hail, Flame who comes backwards, I have not stolen what belongs to the gods.

9.   Hail, Bone-Crusher who comes from Heracleopolis, I have not lied.

10. Hail, Flame-Grower who comes from Memphis, I have not carried away food.

11. Hail, Qerti, who comes from the west, I have not uttered evil words.

12. Hail, Shining-Tooth who comes from Ta-She, I have attacked no man.

13. Hail, Blood-Consumer who comes from the house of slaughter, I have not slaughtered sacred cattle.

14. Hail, Entrail-Consumer who comes from the mabet chamber, I have not cheated.

15. Hail, God of Maat who comes from the city of twin Maati, 10 I have not laid waste lands which have been ploughed.

16. Hail, Backward-Walker who comes from Bubastis, I have not pried mischievously into others' affairs.

17. Hail, Aati who comes from Heliopolis, I have not foolishly set my mouth in motion against another man.

18. Hail, doubly evil who comes from Ati, I have not given way to wrath without cause.

19. Hail, serpent Amenti who comes from the house of slaughter, I have not defiled the wife of a man.

20. Hail, you who look at what is brought to you who comes from the Temple of Amsu, I have not pollluted myself.

21. Hail, Chief of the Princes who comes from Nehatu, I have not terrified any man.

22. Hail, Destroyer who comes from the Lake of Kaui, I have not trespassed sacred grounds.

23. Hail, Speech-Orderer who comes from the Urit, I have not been angry.

24. Hail, Child who comes from the Lake of Heqat, I have not made myself deaf to Maat.

25. Hail, Disposer-of-Speech who comes from Unes, I have not stirred up strife.

26. Hail, Basti who comes from the Secret City, I have made no one to weep.

27. Hail, Backwards-Face who comes from the Dwelling, I have committed no acts of impurity.

28. Hail, Leg-of-Fire who comes from the Akheku, I have not eaten my heart.

29. Hail, Kenemti who comes from Kenemet, I have not abused anyone.

30. Hail, Offering-Bringer who comes from Sais, I have not acted with violence.

31. Hail, Lord-of-Faces who comes from Tchefet, I have not judged hastily.

32. Hail, Giver-of-Knowledge who comes from Unth, I have not taken vengeance on a god.

33. Hail, Lord-of-Two-Horns who comes from Satiu, I have not spoken too much.

34. Hail, Nefer-Tem who comes from Memphis, I have not acted with deceit nor have I performed wickedness.

35. Hail, Tem-Sep who comes from Tattu, I have not cursed the king.

36. Hail, Heart-Laborer who comes from Tebti, I have not polluted the water.

37. Hail, Ahi-of-the-water who comes from Nu, I have not been haughty.

38. Hail, Man-Commander, who comes from Sau, I have not cursed the god.

39. Hail, Neheb-nefert who comes from the Lake of Nefer, I have not been insolent.

40. Hail, Neheb-kau who comes from your city, I have not been sought distinctions.

41. Hail, Holy-Head who comes from your dwelling, I have not increased my wealth, except with such things as were mine.

42. Hail, Arm-Bringer who comes from the the Underworld, I have not scorned the god of my city.

Recommended Reading

Stadler, Martin. (2008). Judgment after Death (Negative Confession). UC Los Angeles: UCLA Encyclopedia of Egyptology.

Jeremy Naydler, *Temple of the Cosmos: The Ancient Egyptian Experience of the Sacred* (Rochester: Inner Traditions, 1996).

Manfred Lurker, *The Gods and Symbols of Ancient Egypt* (London: Thames & Hudson, 1980)

The Leaves Upon the Wind Method

Use the element of Air to Divine your Deck and cast your Question to the Winds

Take the Major Cards (or a picture of same) and fasten each of them to one of 22 balloons. Also fasten a small stamped postcard to the balloon and place your name and address on it and a request to return the postcard. Ensure the postcard has the name or number of the Tarot card on it.

If you are nervous about sending Tarot cards into the air, select 22 postcards whose pictures represent the 22 Majors. This is a fun exercise in itself. Fasten them to the balloons, using a number on the postcard also to remind you which Tarot card it represents.

Consider your question and release the balloons into the air at a propitious moment. You will of course realize that if doing this with an original deck, you may not see some of these cards again.

As the cards come back to you through the postal system, read them as an answer to your question. The delays between the returns or the lack of return of some, all or any card is also a divinatory response. You may also get messages written on your return cards, such as "This was found upside down in my pond in Carlisle" signifying the card is reversed and the meaning of the card is where you can find strength (the place-name Carlisle comes from the Latin for "fort").

Illus. Balloons.

The 4MAT® Spread

A spread for learning best from a dramatic event of the past or future.

The 4MAT® cycle is a system of learning and teaching using 4 quadrants of a circle and is a useful model for all teachers and trainers – even Tarot teachers! Here in this simple 4-card spread we use it to explore how we might learn from a powerful event in our own lives.

Draw 4 Cards.

1. What was really going on in the **experience**?

2. What can we learn from **reflecting** on the experience?

3. How can we **learn** from, comprehend our reflection, make sense of it?

4. How can we **act** on what we have learnt?

You can also consider the base card (the card at the bottom of the deck when you have performed this reading) as the **integration** card, showing you how this event fits into the rest of your life.

You can perform this spread as a predictive or coaching spread about a major event in the life of a Querent, such as an important job start, change of location, relationship etc., to ensure they get the best out of the change to come.

A Note For Tarot Teachers

You can learn more about Bernice McCarthy's 4MAT® cycle at her blog and the site http://www.aboutlearning.com.

I would also recommend her book, with Dennis McCarthy, *Teaching around the 4MAT cycle: designing instruction for diverse learners* (Thousand Oaks, CA: Corwin Press, 2006).

The GO Method

A method for divining how two parties will develop together for better or worse.

The Game of GO has been played for thousands of years and with elegant simplicity, its rules generate a beautiful pattern of play which reflects life. Indeed, as said by one Japanese *Noh* poet, the "white and black stones become the colors of night and day" and the 360 intersections of a full game board become the "numbers of the days of the year".

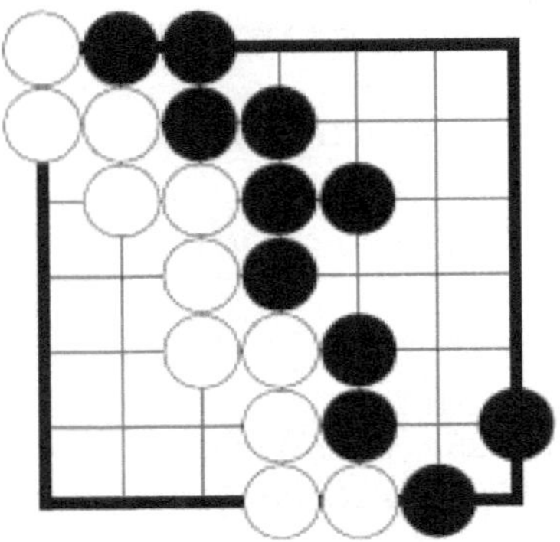

Illus. A Small GO Board.

In fact, in connection with cards, there is an 1811 bible which has as a frontispiece text a discussion between a soldier and a mayor, the latter of whom has caught the solider with a deck of cards in church. The soldier, in his defense, relates how a deck of playing cards is not a sin but rather an almanac of the world and the bible. This includes "when I count how many spots there are in a pack of cards I find there are three hundred and sixty-five. There are so many days in year". The Mayor points out this is a mistake, but the soldier answers it is impossible to create a perfect almanac in every respect – something we saw in **Tarot Timings** earlier!

As play proceeds in GO, there are seen to be arising strategic patterns and flows of moves, creating constellations of stones in play with evocative names such as "ladder", "net" or "carpenters' box". We use this element of GO in our Tarot method of reading.

This works best on a GO board, or a chessboard or other matrix pattern, such as the black and white chequers on a decorated tabletop. It uses two decks. In my example, I chose the **PSYCARDS** and the **UNIVERSAL WAITE** decks.

To perform a reading using the GO Method:

1. Choose which deck will represent each party.

2. Shuffle both decks.

3. Lay down the first card from one of the decks. This is the first position of the first party and indicates their current state.

4. Lay down anywhere on the board the first card from the second deck. This is the first position of the second party and indicates their current state.

5. Now select the next card from the first deck and place it to respond to the previous card "played". You may feel as if you should lay it close to the one of the two cards in play, or not, perhaps between them.

6. Allow the cards and positions to suggest the arising play. This is a purely intuitive method and the aim should be to create subtle patterns of meaning and interpretation during the play of the cards.

7. If a number of cards surround a card, then the central card(s) might be removed, showing how the influence of one party acts upon the other.

Sometimes you might find yourself running cards in a straight line, called a ladder in GO. This shows certain inevitability in the situation.

You may create rules as you progress, such as if the *Blasted Tower* is played close to any other card from the other deck, that other card is immediately removed from the board and annulled from the situation.

Recommended Reading & Resources

GO! More Than a Game, Peter Shotwell (Boston, Tuttle Publishing, 2003).

Psycards at http://www.psycards.com

Illus. Preparing Psycards and Tarot Cards on a GO Board.

The Stairway to Heaven Spread [Narrative Method]

A Narrative spread of Tarosophy for divining the nature of our own spiritual ascent.

Illus. Ramon Lull (Ladder of Ascent, 1512).

Placed edge to edge, they form, as it were, a symbolic ladder leading from Heaven to earth. From the summit of this ladder God, the Prima Causa, governs the world - not directly, but stepwise, ex gradibus, by means of a succession of intermediaries. The divine power is thus transmitted down to the lowest level of humanity, to the humble beggar. But the ladder can likewise be read from bottom to top; seen in this way it 'teaches that man may gradually raise himself in the spiritual order, reaching at last the heights of the Bonum, the Veram, and the Nobile - and that science and virtue bring him closer to God.

The *Survival of the Pagan Gods*, Jean Seznac, describing the Tarocchi of Mantegna [ca. 1460] pp. 138 - 139.

In this method, we insert Tarot cards into a narrative flow of text to create a journal entry for contemplation. Simply read out or write the narrative and select cards as you work through the narrative.

This particular narrative is designed from the writings of Saint John Climacus, *The Ladder of Ascent*. It uses 30 cards. You may also derive suitable narratives from any other religious or meaningful text, such as the Charge of the Goddess by Doreen Valiente (following this example), the *Holy Books of Thelema*, or other mystical verse or poetry.

On renunciation of the world … I will work on [card 1]

On detachment … I will examine my attachment to [card 2]

On exile or pilgrimage; concerning dreams that beginners have … I will consider [card 3]

On blessed and ever-memorable obedience (in addition to episodes involving many individuals) … I will ensure [card 4]

On painstaking and true repentance which constitutes the life of the holy convicts; and about the Prison … I will think upon [card 5]

On remembrance of death … [card 6]

On joy-making and mourning … I will be reminded of [card 7]

On freedom from anger and on meekness … I will [card 8]

On remembrance of wrongs … I must [card 9]

On slander or calumny … it is seen that [card 10]

On talkativeness and silence … the importance is [card 11]

On lying … there is only [card 12]

On despondency … the lesson is [card 13]

On that clamorous mistress, the stomach … we see [card 14]

On incorruptible purity and chastity, to which the corruptible attain by toil and sweat … we are taught [card 15]

On love of money, or avarice … I know [card 16]

On non-possessiveness (that hastens one Heavenwards) … [card 17]

On insensibility, that is, deadening of the soul and the death of the mind before the death of the body … I believe [card 18]

On sleep, prayer, and psalmody with the brotherhood ... there is [card 19]

On bodily vigil and how to use it to attain spiritual vigil, and how to practice it ... [card 20]

On unmanly and puerile cowardice ... avoided by [card 21]

On the many forms of vainglory ... we must reason [card 22]

On mad pride and (in the same Step) on unclean blasphemous thoughts; concerning unmentionable blasphemous thoughts ... [card 23]

On meekness, simplicity, and guilelessness which come not from nature but from conscious effort, and about guile ... the lesson is [card 24]

On the destroyer of the passions, most sublime humility, which is rooted in spiritual perception ... I come to know [card 25]

On discernment of thoughts, passions and virtues; on expert discernment; brief summary of all aforementioned ... the outcome is [card 26]

On holy stillness of body and soul; different aspects of stillness and how to distinguish them ... I learn [card 27]

On holy and blessed prayer, the mother of virtues, and on the attitude of mind and body in prayer ... from which I take [card 28]

Concerning Heaven on earth, or Godlike dispassion and perfection, and the resurrection of the soul before the general resurrection ... this means to me [card 29]

Concerning the linking together of the supreme trinity among the virtues; a brief exhortation summarizing all that has said at length in this text ... the outcome is [card 30].

The Cards of the Goddess [Narrative Spread]

A narrative spread based on the Charge of the Goddess by Doreen Valiente.

In this pagan spread, we examine our relationship to Nature and the divine Goddess. There are of course many pagan-based or Witchcraft and Wiccan decks that are suitable for this particular method. This method makes for a wonderful entry in your *Book of Shadows*. It is based on Doreen Valiente's *Charge of the Goddess*:

> Whenever ye have need of any thing, once in the month, and better it be when the moon is full, then shall ye assemble in some secret place and adore the spirit of She, who is Queen of all witches. There shall ye assemble, ye who are fain to learn all sorcery, yet have not won its deepest secrets; to these will She teach things that are yet unknown. And ye shall be free from slavery; and as a sign that ye be really free, ye shall be naked in your rites; and ye shall dance, sing, feast, make music and love, all in Her praise. For Hers is the ecstasy of the spirit, and Hers also is joy on earth; for Her law is love unto all beings. Keep pure your highest ideal; strive ever towards it; let naught stop you or turn you aside. For Hers is the secret door which opens upon the land of youth and Hers is the cup of wine of life, and the cauldron of Cerridwen, which is the Holy Grail of immortality. She is the gracious goddess, who gives the gift of joy unto the heart of man. Upon earth, She gave the knowledge of the spirit eternal; and beyond death, She gives peace and freedom, and reunion with those who have gone before.

Nor does She demand sacrifice, for behold, She is the mother of all living, and Her love is poured out upon the earth.

She who is the beauty of the green earth, and the white moon among the stars, and the mystery of the waters, and the desire of the heart of man, calls unto thy soul. Arise, and come unto Her. For She is the soul of nature, who gives life to the universe. from Her all things proceed, and unto Her all things must return; and before Her face, beloved of gods and men, let thine innermost divine self be enfolded in the rapture of the infinite. Let Her worship be within the heart that rejoiceth; for behold, all acts of love and pleasure are Her rituals. And therefore let there be beauty and strength, power and compassion, honor and humility, mirth and reverence within you. And thou who thinkest to seek Her, know thy seeking and yearning shall avail thee not unless thou knowest the mystery; that if that which thou seekest thou findest not within thee, then thou wilt never find it without thee. For behold, She has been with thee from the beginning; and She is that which is attained at the end of desire.

☽○☾

I [magical/pagan name] declare to the Goddess of my need [card 1]. I honor you with [card 2] once in the month, and better it be when the moon is full, for I value in others [card 3] and my secret place is [card 4].

I adore you for [card 5], Queen of all witches. I learn in my sorcery that [card 6] and its deepest secret, [card 7]. Teach me to know further about [card 8].

I shall be free of [card 9] and be more open in my [card 10]. I shall find enjoyment in [card 11]. I shall seek ecstasy and love in [card 12].

Let me see my highest ideal in [card 13] and strive ever towards it. I will not be stopped by [card 14]. The secret door is found in [card 15] and the wine of life is [card 16].

The mysteries of Life and Death are [card 17 + card 18] and held by you. My sacrifice is [card 19] yet of this you do not demand.

In the mysteries of Nature, we learn [card 20 + card 21 + card 22].

Your beauty is [card 23] and I am called to you by [card 24]. You are the Soul of Nature, the [card 24] and your face is bloved of Gods and Men. My inner self will be revealed in [card 25] and enfolded in your rapture.

I will worship you with [card 26] and find strength in [card 27] and compassion in [card 28]. Your rituals are [card 29] and the mystery within me is revealed as [card 30]. You are [card 31] and have been with me from the beginning. The end of my desire is [card 32].

☽〇☾

You can try this narrative as a *split-spread* with the Major cards only for the first 22 cards and the Minors only for the remaining 10 cards. You can add Court cards if you are comfortable with applying their meanings in this type of narrative.

Here is an example of applying various cards from the **Otherworld Tarot** (Williams & Nowell, pub. Schiffer, 2010) to the narrative, which contain keywords on the cards to assist reading.

> "I will worship you with [Tower/**New Way of Life**] making those changes in my life which seem striking at the moment, clearing away the debris of the past and find strength in [Knight of Swords/**Change through Conflict**] the inevitable change which will bring me into conflict with others. I will find compassion by [Six of Pentacles/**Sharing**] sharing this journey with others and writing about it for all to see."

The One Year to Live Spread

A Self-discovery spread based on living a year as if it were your last.

Begin this exercise with a moment's consideration and the scenario that you have been given an accurate prognosis of your death, in exactly one year from this moment. You then shuffle the deck and select 12 cards, one relating to each month and the consideration of that month.

You can perform this spread as an exercise or to prepare 12 cards for your "Contemplation Card of the Month" each month for the year following the reading. In this example I have used the months January to December for convenience.

January: What is my initial reaction?

February: How do I prepare for death?

March: How do I live and heal?

April: How do I live each day?

May: How do I review my life?

June: How do I offer service?

July: Who dies?

August: What is beyond my death?

September: How do I leave my body and belongings?

October: What message do I leave behind?

November: What is change?

December: How do I die?

This is a profound reading and is worthy of your time to consider its results and place them in a journal. You may wish to revisit this reading on occasion and add further notes over time.

This reading is unique in that the first time performed; it provides the immediate answers for unlocking in your life. If you perform it again, it is never the same as the first reading, like hearing a joke for the second time or watching the same film again, knowing the surprise finale.

Recommended Reading

Stephen Levine, *A Year to Live: How to Live this Year as if it were your Last* (Crown Publishing, 1998).

Interview at: http://www.personaltransformation.com/Levine.html

Branching Spread Method

A basic fractal spread to explore a situation as you wish, based on the cards drawn.

Consider the Querent's question and shuffle - or have them shuffle. Lay down 4 cards from the deck face up in a vertical line.

Read the four cards as the basic essence of the situation. Then decide (or have the Querent ask) which area of that you wish to explore and to which card that area relates.

Lay two further cards branching out from that card as in the diagram. Read these as further aspects highlighting that area of the reading. You can then further branch out from either of those cards or return to another area of the trunk with new information, and branch out again.

Illus. Branching Spread Method.

Always return to the central trunk of cards if you get lost performing this type of reading and return to the essential question.

The Dice Man Method

A Tarot Method for entering a realm of madness and returning slightly more whole.

... on the other hand, if you want a friend, go out of your way to agree enthusiastically with his passionately held belief. Soon he will barely be able to restrain himself from embracing you. It is such a treat for him to have reality patting him on the back instead of rattling his shell. The fact that you are faking it never enters his mind. Since his belief is Truth, it is only natural that you should agree with him.

> Luke Rhinehart, *The Book of the Die* (London: HarperCollins, 2000) p.128

1. Roll a dice twice and add up the two numbers.

2. Take your Tarot deck and shuffle.

3. Select out the number of cards indicated by the dice.

4. Look at each card and assign to it an arbitrary but possible action, behavior or experience appropriate to the card.

For example:

a. 8 of Wands = Take a Flight Somewhere.

b. 7 of Swords = Go dancing or fencing.

c. 4 of Cups = Join a meditation class or go to a Yoga Lesson.

d. Page of Pentacles = Go to a weights lesson in a gym.

e. Wheel of Fortune = Go visit a Casino or Las Vegas.

Now simply shuffle those cards and select one out.

You have one week in which to perform that action.

Repeat as often as you require.

Anima/Animus Spread

A layout exploring the masculine and feminine energies within the Tarot.

A layout is a particular arrangement of the Tarot to demonstrate a particular pattern, sequence or different energies. It is often composed of the 22 Major Arcana arranged in lines of particular length, a circle, or similar. Sometimes the layout is designed based on correspondences such as Astrology or Kabbalah.

In this layout, we explore the Jungian concept of Anima and Animus through a layout of Tarot cards which correspond to aspects of that concept. This leads us to particular way of viewing male and female energies as embodied by our Tarot deck. As with all layouts, the intention is to open our perception to a deeper view of the world whilst also enabling us to have more depth when performing readings.

In simple terms, the *anima* the feminine quality within the masculine, and the *animus* is the masculine quality in the feminine. Jung considered "the encounter with the shadow is the 'apprentice-piece' in the individual's development. ... that with the anima [animus] is the 'masterpiece'".[3]

In Jung's view, both anima and animus in all individuals have four distinct levels of development, leading the masculine and feminine individual to an increasing sensitivity and spiritual awareness:

- Eve – the female seen as the object of desire
- Helen – the female seen as self-reliant
- Mary – the female seen as virtuous
- Sophia – the female seen as an individual

The animus also has four levels:

- Physical Power

[3] Jung quoted in Anthony Stevens *On Jung* (London 1990) p. 206.

- Man of Action – Romantic or Hunter
- The bearer of the word – an Orator
- The incarnation of meaning – a spiritual mediator

In both cases, for the individual pursuing individuation, working to integrate their anima or animus – which Jung called the "masterpiece" of one's life work - leads to an encounter with the archetypal wise old woman or wise old man.

To explore this layout, simply go through the Major 22 Arcana and lay out the cards you believe to represent the 4 stages of Anima and Animus Development. At the top of each, place the card you see as representing the Wise Old Man and Wise Old Woman.

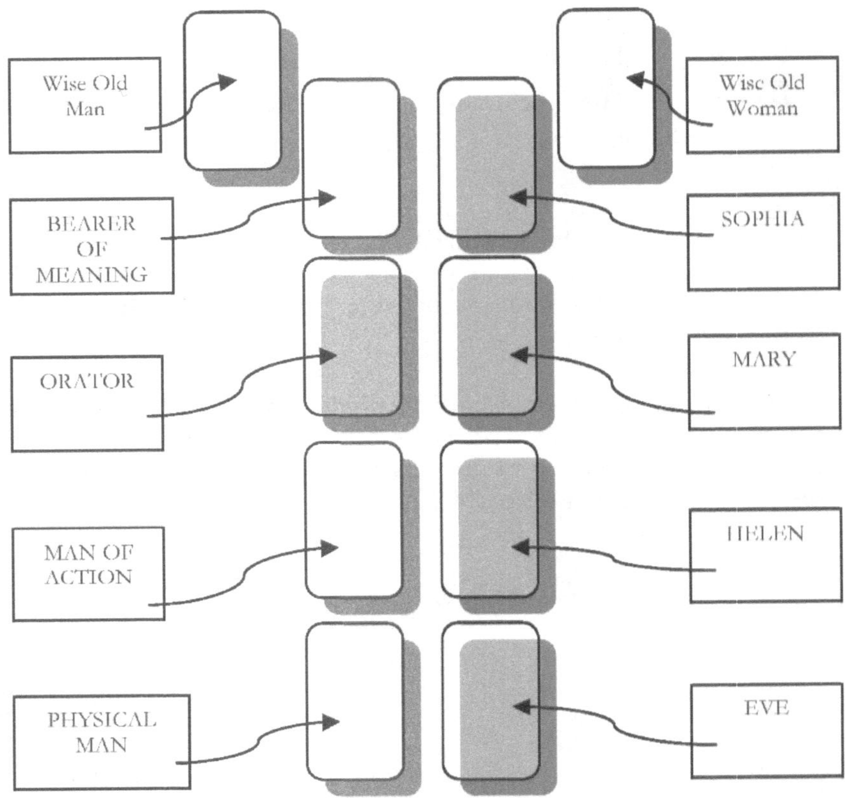

Illus. Anima/Animus Layout.

You can now compare the meanings you have for these cards in the pairs that you have placed them. What does this tell you about how you relate to those aspects of yourself – and when you find that in others?

Buffers & Shocks (4th Way Method)

A Fourth Way Tarot method where we observe what separates us from the real world.

In the work of the mystic G. I. Gurdjieff, he proposed that each of us has a *Kundabuffer*, an organ "to prevent men seeing the reality of their situation". Whilst this was proposed in a semi-fictional sense (as much of Gurdjieff's writings) it is an important concept in self-awareness work.

One way of seeing the kundabuffers is that they are the psychological defense mechanisms that connect and absorb the minor shock of our ever-changing sense of self from one identity or personality to another. Usually in our day we ride these shocks on an almost momentary basis as we change our state and role. The **Fourth Way** of Gurdjieff promotes observation of these shocks to wake us up to the reality of our situation.

In this method, we use Tarot to firstly elicit the nature of these buffers, and then prompt awareness and self-remembering.

Lay out 4 cards:

1. This is when I lie to myself or others.

2. This is when I suppress what I feel.

3. This is when I identify with a role.

4. This is when I project onto others.

Read the cards and make interpretation. When you have done so, decide which one Kundabuffer you would like to work with, and select a further *recall card* in answer to this statement, "When I see this card I will see myself [lying / suppressing / Identifying / projecting] and remember myself."

Now take an image of that particular *recall card* – or the card itself – and ensure it is about your person for a week. Everytime you see it, use it as a shock to alert you as to whether you are experiencing full awareness, or caught in your Kundabuffer. Affter the week is over, return to the first card you selected for that Kundabuffer and re-intrepret it.

Recommended Reading

Charles T. Tart, *Waking Up* (Longmead: Element Books, 1988).

Nine Swords Spread (Way of Grief)

A short spread to work with loss and grief in all its forms.

Lay out the Nine of Swords in the Waite-Smith Tarot.

Beneath it lay out nine cards (one for every Sword) showing the nature of the loss and what has befallen the Querent. Then point out that in the card, the figure cannot see an end to any Sword – a point.

Then lay out another column of nine cards to show the inevitable point for each of the Swords of Grief.

Signal to Noise Method (Clarification Spread)

A method of cutting to the chase of a situation.

In this simple *Twist* method, we perform any standard spread. This tells us the situation as it appears to be presenting itself. However, we then deem that situation as manifesting a more profound communication – a lesson to ourselves from the Universe itself.

We then re-shuffle the deck and lay a card on top of every card already laid down in the spread, with the following context:

If that first reading was the **noise**, this reading is the **signal**.

We then read each of the cards in the context of the one below it, regarding the position in the spread. Thus, for example in the 15-card spread called variously the Golden Dawn method, the Thoth Deck method, the Romany Method or the English Method, we have three cards as showing the "influences and events" in the situation.

If these were the Queen of Wands, The Magician and the Wheel of Fortune, we might read that as indicating that the influence on the situation is one of control; that the Querent is going to have to learn to take their vision and ambition (Queen of Wands) and manage their resources (Magician) whilst change takes place (Wheel).

However, this is just the **noise** – the **signal**, when we lay out three cards on top of those, is Knight of Pentacles, Page of Pentacles, 9 of Pentacles. It shows that really what is going to happen is that the Querent is being taught to be patient (Knight of Pentacles), work with what they have got (Page of Pentacles) and be content (9 of Pentacles). In effect, a "get real" signal is underneath the noise of the situation.

Stages of Alchemy Spreads

A Reading to transmute the dull Lead of life into the very uncommon Gold of the Soul.

In this reading we take a dull and dead life situation and transform it into the "uncommon gold" of the Alchemists, through a sequence of alchemical processes. This is ideal when the Querent or oneself does not have a particular question but is feeling somewhat stuck, bored or lifeless.

Consider the situation which is currently the "lead" of life. Shuffle.

Select 7 cards and lay them out in a line. These indicate the divination of seven alchemical processes in sequence:

1. Calcination

2. Solution

3. Coagulation

4. Sublimation

5. Mortification

6. Separation

7. Conjunction

You may also choose to lay out a card above each of these to show the nature of the work required in that phase, and indeed a further row of seven cards to show the results of each stage.

The cards indicate the the way in which you can use alchemy to transform that area of your life into a more spiritual connection:

1. Calcination – What work must I do here?

2. Solution – What am I really seeing here?

3. Coagulation – What is the reality of this situation?

4. Sublimation – How can I elevate this work?

5. Mortification – What must be destroyed and transformed?

6. Separation – What can I take from this time?

7. Conjunction – How can I connect it to what follows?

Recommended Reading

Edward F. Edinger, *Anatomy of the Psyche: Alchemical Symbolism in Psychotherapy* (Chicago: Open Court, 1985).

Yellow Brick Road Spread [Pulled Spread Method]

An example of a pulled spread which is useful for divining a stuck situation.

In *Tarosophy* we use a whole range of new and particular **types** of spreads to suit the question being asked. One of these is the *pulled* spread. This is a spread that is laid out in different directions on a table (sometimes in 3d using Perspex platforms – this works very well with the **Transparent Tarot** or **Transparent Oracle,** pub. Schiffer) and you can see an illustration of this in *Tarosophist International #2.*

This particular example of a pulled spread is themed around *The Wonderful Wizard of Oz* by L. Frank Baum (1900). However, like all the material in *Twist*, it has a deeper significance, in fact eliciting a solution strategy using all aspects of the unconscious processes.

Take a significator card. If you do not use significators, select the Fool card for your Querent or yourself. It helps if the card has a white dog.

Lay that down and say, "This is you/me as Dorothy".

Then lay out three cards face-down in a triangle around the Dorothy card. These represent the LION, the SCARECROW, and the TIN MAN.

Ask the Querent/yourself, "Which way to Oz?" Select one of the three routes and companions. Turn over that card and read it as "This is what will happen". Now lay two new cards face-up next to the other two characters/routes and say, "This is what pulls you elsewhere".

Next ask again, "Which way to Oz?" and select one of the routes again, either continuing down the same yellow brick road, or starting a new one by laying out a new card there. You then lay out one card again for the other two non-chosen routes for "This is what pulls you elsewhere". You can continue this reading until you feel it reaches a conclusion.

To explore this reading more deeply, consider:

- Lion = Will/Courage
- Tin Man = Mind/Thought
- Scarecrow = Heart/Emotions.

Recommended Reading

Neil Eskelin, *What to Do When You Don't Know What to Do* (London: Catalyst, 1995)

Infinity Method (Hebrew One-Card Spread)

Hebrew Depth-Charge the Majors and Read Forever with Just One Card.

In this advanced method, we look at the correspondences to one Card and take advantage of a peculiar aspect of Hebrew, in that Hebrew letters are also spelt as words. This reflects a Kabbalistic teaching that each *Sephirah* on the Tree of Life contains another Tree of Life, reaching on to infinity – a fractal property. We can find this fractal property in our Tarot.

Certain mathematical formulae involving complex numbers composed of both real numbers and imaginary numbers (such as i, which is the symbol denoting the square root of -1) can produce graphs such as the Mandelbrot set which have recursive properties, that is, they repeat their patterns at lower or higher orders of complexity and calculation. Thus, when magnifying, mathematically, an area of the Mandelbrot set, one can find the same strange shape emerging, and within certain areas of that shape, the shape repeats, and so forth.

This discovery reminds us of the Kabbalistic doctrine of Sephiroth existing within Sephiroth. Indeed, Joseph ibn Sayyah went as far as to describe in detail the play of lights within the Sephiroth to the fourth degree, as, for example, the "Tiferet which is in Gedullah which is in Binah which is in Keter".

Again, this finds a similarity with one eastern concept which states that "there is no beginning, no ending, no linear progression, only an unbounded net of jewels each of which reflects and contains the reflection of each of the others".

Thus, the repetitive plan which is spoken of in Kabbalah, and the fact that each Sephirah "contains the other nine", is due to the fractal or recursive nature of the Kabbalistic system symbolized by the Tree of Life, and referred to often as the Orchard of Trees.

Another technological advance which resumes this idea is that of hologram images, which are produced by projecting the interference patterns made by light waves (lasers) about an object onto photographic plate.

Shining light on the plate from the same angle then produces the image of the object from the viewer's location. As Itzhak Bentov explains, if one were to freeze such an interference pattern, for example, the ripples in water made by a stone being dropped, then one could, analyzing the pattern, discover where the stone had broken through the water. On a note of poetic whimsy, one could perhaps visualize the Tree of Life as the wave-front of the light of God.

One may realize that all the above modern ideas are actually pre-empted and summarized in a more ancient doctrine, which states, in the *Tabula Smaragdina* (Table of Emerald); "It is true without lying, certain and most true, that which is inferior or below, is as that which is superior, or above, and that which is superior as that which is inferior, to work and accomplish the miracles of one thing."

Patterns emerge at all levels and all scales, such as the spiral of a shell and the spiral of a fern branch, or the shape of a galaxy and the shape of a human cell. As Louise B. Young states in the *Unfinished Universe*, "the whole is imminent in all the parts, no matter how small". To those who work with such a self-reflexive system, then it becomes possible to model, and experience, states that often defy description in other, more linear systems. As Blake puts it in "Auguries of Innocence"

"To see a World in a grain of sand,

And a heaven in a wild flower,

Hold infinity in the palm of your hand,

And eternity in an hour"

Such is the promise that the Tree of Sapphires (another translation of the word *Sephirah*) holds, as each facet of each sapphire reflects eternally upon each other in a labyrinth of light.

With that text in mind, we now look at how we can take advantage of this fractal nature in our Tarot, via the magic of correspondence. I first reproduce a table of the correspondences for the Major Arcana which we use in this one card reading method.

This table also shows the full spelling in transliteration of each letter.

Letter	Letter	Letter in full	Tarot Card
Aleph	A	ALPh	0 : FOOL
Beth	B	BYTh	I : MAGICIAN
Gimel	G	GML (GYML)	II : PRIESTESS
Daleth	D	DLTh	III : EMPRESS
Heh	H	HA	IV : EMPEROR
Vau	V	VV	V : HIEROPHANT
Zain	Z	ZYN	VI : LOVERS
Cheth	Ch	ChYTh	VII : CHARIOT
Teth	T	TYTh	VIII : STRENGTH
Yod	Y	YVD	IX : HERMIT
Kaph	K	KPh	X : WHEEL
Lamed	L	LMD	XI : JUSTICE
Mem	M	MYM	XII : HANGED MAN
Nun	N	NVN	XIII : DEATH
Samekh	S	SMKh	XIV : TEMPERANCE
Ayin	A'a	AYN	XV : DEVIL
Peh	Ph	PhA, PhY or PhH	XVI : TOWER
Tzaddi	Tz	TzDY	XVII : STAR
Qoph	Q	QVPh	XVIII : MOON
Resh	R	RYSh	XIX : SUN
Shin	Sh	ShYN	XX : LAST JUDGEMENT
Tau	Th	TV	XXI : UNIVERSE

With this table you can now depth-charge your one card reading with a single Major Arcana card.

Select out the 22 Major Arcana. Consider your question or the Querent's question and draw a single card. In this example, we will use the HERMIT. We read the first card as the **literal or surface** answer, so we interpret this as indicating the questioner needs to take time to themselves.

We then look at the corresponding letter, in this case, Yod. This is transliterated as "Y" but is spelt in full as YVD. Looking these letters up, we see that they are Yod – Vau – and Daleth.

We now select the cards corresponding to that spelling – Hermit (again), Hierophant and Empress. This gives us the next level of reading, which is the **symbolic** nature of the answer. In this case, we are not literal, we take the cards as symbols showing the person must allow the environment to take care of itself (Empress), must seek expert advice (Hierophant) and keep to their own path (Hermit).

Now we have the cards for YVD, we can see that Yod, Vau and Daleth each have their own spellings, so we can fractal downwards:

Y   =   YVD   = Hermit, Hierophant, Empress

V   =   VV   = Hierophant, Hierophant

D   =   DLTh   = Empress, Justice, World

Now we have an **extended** answer, which is the deeper call or mythic nature of the situation. Here we see from the Hermit at the top we always come down to a deeper call about finding revelation and justice in the world. You will notice that the Hierophant is now represented three times in the eight cards at this level.

And of course, we can now see why this spread is called the infinity method. Each of the letters still has its own spelling in full. So we can further go down – just one more level to gain the **secret** answer - for our purposes – as follows:

YVD   =   YVD + VV + DLTh

VV   =   VV + VV

DLTh   =   DLTh + LMD + ThV

So those are the cards (from the letters on the right) ... Hermit Hierophant Empress (YVD) + Hierophant Hierophant (VV) + Empress

Justice World (DLTh) + Hierophant Hierophant (VV) + Empress Justice World (DLTh) + Justice Hanged Man Empress (LMD) + World Hierophant (ThV).

Something interesting has happened now at our secret level to the Hermit card – we have the same letters (and cards) recurring as our previous levels, with one exception – the HANGED MAN (Mem).

At a secret level, the Hanged Man is found four layers below the Hermit. Perhaps this signifies that when we turn to ourselves through the Hermit, we connect to our highest values and see the world differently as does the Hanged Man.

Radiance Method

A simple method to discover how you or your Querent will shine from a reading.

If the Sun card appears in a reading, consult the card or pair of cards either side of the Sun to indicate how the Querent or yourself might shine from receiving this reading.

If the Sun card has not appeared in the reading, go through the deck and discover the Sun card and consult the two cards either side of it.

You can of course do this with any other Major Arcana card, to discover how the Querent might **reflect** on the reading (from the Moon cards location and two cards either side), how the Querent might take **control** (Magician card) and so forth.

The Mason's Spread

A secret spread of Masonic import which answers the question "How?"

In this spread, we look at answering the fundamental question proposed with "How do I ...?" for example, "How do I go about getting my life back on track?" or "How do I get the most out of the new job?"

The spread is a simple layout spread using the concept of the Masons Tools.

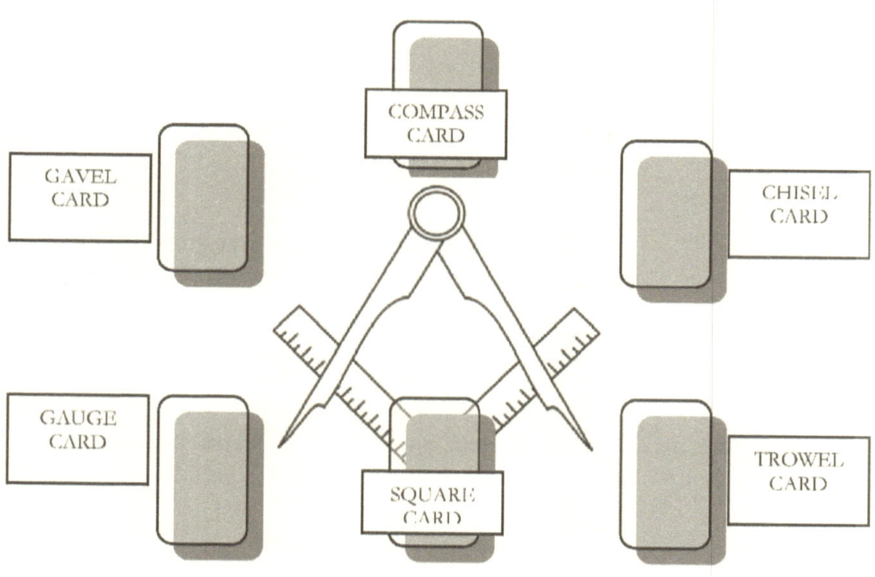

Illus. Mason's Spread.

1. **The Compass Card** shows the way in which the persons spirit can be brought into action in this matter.

2. **The Square Card** shows the environment and how that can be manipulated to bring about change in the situation.

3. **The Gavel Card** shows the active will which can be brought to bear.

4. **The Chisel Card** shows where the passive force will bring results by letting things go in that particular area or delegating, giving control away.

5. **The Gauge Card** indicates the likely success or outcome of the action.

6. **The Trowel Card** shows the first step or action that must be taken.

Recommended Reading

Daniel Beresniak, *Symbols of Freemasonry* (New York: Assouline, 2000).

SNAP Method

Using Two Decks to get a Second Opinion or Confirmation Reading

Ever been unsure as to a reading? If you have a second deck you can try this simple confirmation method. Whilst the Oracles are sometimes tricky when you ask them time and time again, this method goes some way to providing a second opinion.

This works with 5-7 card readings. If they are smaller or larger, the figures just will not work so clearly although you might find ways to take this into account.

Take your original spread (5-7 cards) and lay out the cards in a straight line. Then contemplate these cards and your original interpretation and shuffle the second deck. Lay out the same number of cards below the original spread.

For every card which is the same in both readings, in the same position, statistically unlikely, award yourself 10 points. For every card which is the same, but in a different position, award yourself 5 points. For every Suit or Number, the same in both rows (whatever their position) award yourself 2 points. If you have the same Court Card in both lines that counts for 4 points.

If you have the same Major card in both readings, award yourself 20 points. If it is in the same position, the reading should be considered clearly confirmed in its original reading.

About 20 points of similarity are more than enough to confirm a reading, however, if there are no points at all, that might mean your original reading should be replaced by the second reading.

I did this recently with an online spread with regard to a relationship question. I got 14 points total similarity between two readings for the same question, however, 10 points of which was the 2 of Cups appearing in the same position ("How the other person considers the relationship"). I took this to indicate that whether I was sure or not about the reading or my interpretation, the other person certainly knew their mind. The practice of Tarot reading is an imperfect science but a perfect art.

SUNSET SPREAD

A straightforward evening review spread to accompany the Dawn Spread.

I (Marcus) designed the Dawn spread, which features in the Courtyard Course of Tarot Professionals and Tarot-Town, in September 1983, when I was 18, almost 30 years ago. I was shocked to see my original notes for it in my first Tarot journal recently!

So, I decided to return to that original concept – a simple spread for the "Day Ahead" type practice readings, with a **Sunset Spread**, for reviewing the Day. This - like the Dawn Spread - is an ideal Journaling Spread.

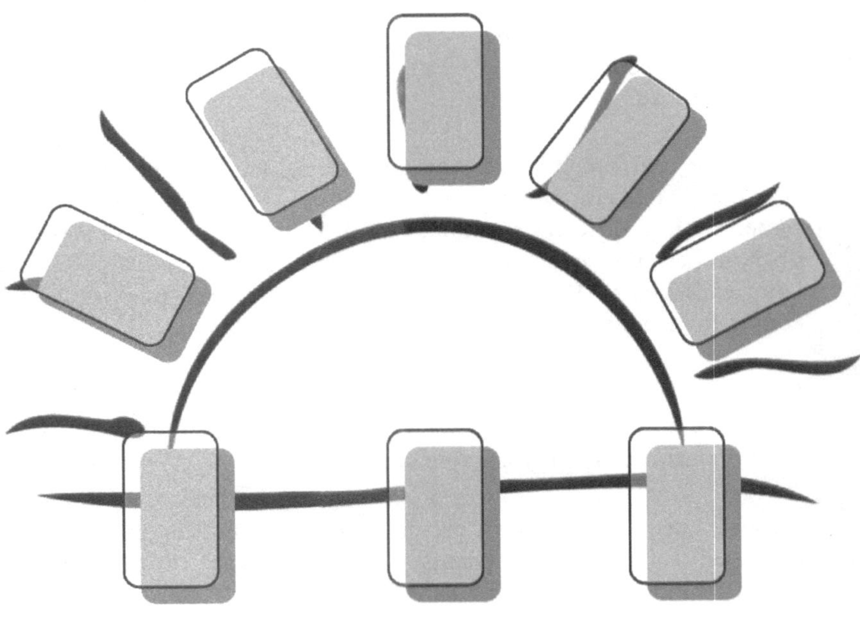

Illus. The Sunset Spread.

The 3 Base cards:

1. Review – What is the basic lesson I can take from today?

2. Resolve – What do I need to do differently tomorrow?

3. Refine – What can I see now that I could not see before?

The 5 Arched cards:

1. Others – What have I learnt about those around me?

2. Environment – What have I learnt about the world?

3. Me – What can I say about myself now?

4. Problems – What is the nature of the challenges I face?

5. Solution – Where shall I look for solutions tomorrow?

THE ALCHEMISTS SPREAD

A spiritual visualization into the Alchemical plane using Tarot.

The introduction of Alchemy to the western tradition can be precisely dated to 11th February, 1144, when Robert of Chester's "Book of the Composition of Alchemy" was published. This book was part of a new current of free-thinkers, bringing Islamic thought to the West, such as Adelard of Bath. As such, alchemy was already proving significant in cross-fertilising philosophies between east and west. Alchemy was also a publishing endeavor; more books on alchemy were published in England between 1650 and 1680 than before or afterwards.

Alchemy is concerned with both exterior and interior, hence the acronymic motto; VITRIOL, *Visita Interiora Terrae Rectificando Invenies Occultum Lapidem* which translates to: "Visit the interior of the earth by rectification you will find the hidden stone". In this it is identical to Asana, which is not merely physical position of the body, but the inherently associated and corresponding change in awareness that comes from physical changes. The word asana is derived from the Sanskrit verb 'Aas' which means existence and state of existence is Asana or Position. Here the position of Body as well as Mind is expected in Asana.

Alchemy is rife with complex and mysterious symbolism. As Norton wrote,

> "Also, they wrote not every man to teach
>
> But to show themselves by secret speech.
>
> Whereby each of his fellows were made certain:
>
> how that he was to them a brother,
>
> For every of them understood another."[4]

---

[4] Quoted in Carl Henrich, *Strange Fruit* (London: Bloomsbury, 1995), p. 40. Originally from Norton, Theatr. Chem. 'Ordinall' p. 40.

Illus. The Stages of Alchemy.

It is not just the spiritual realm to which Alchemy significantly provides a bridge, but the psychological realm. Jung wrote, "Alchemy, therefore, has performed for me the great and invaluable service of providing material in which my experience could find sufficient room."[5]

One of the most significant utilizations of alchemy in the western esoteric tradition is as a model of the initiation system. Although various alchemical authors describe different stages, steps, phases and orders of transformation and transmutation in their works, the significance of a perceivable pattern of progress is an essential underpinning to the organization of many esoteric orders. This progress is often measured in the ten 'grades' corresponding to the Tree of Life, although the alchemical process is more often than not modeled in 7, 9 or 12 steps.

Here are George Ripley's twelve stages:

- The First Gate - Calcination

- The Second Gate - Solution

- The Third Gate - Separation

- The Fourth Gate - Conjunction

- The Fifth Gate - Putrefaction

- The Sixth Gate - Congelation

- The Seventh Gate - Cibation

- The Eighth Gate - Sublimation

- The Ninth Gate - Fermentation

---

[5] Edward F. Edinger, *Anatomy of the Psyche: Alchemical Symbolism in Psychotherapy* (Illinois: Open Court Press, 1994), p. 2. This is quoted from Jung, CW 14, para. 792, but Edinger's book gives a clearer depiction of the stages of alchemy corresponding to the individuation process, and hence, to some degree, the initiation system of the esoteric tradition.

- The Tenth Gate - Exaltation

- The Eleventh Gate - Multiplication

- The Twelfth Gate - Projection

The first two stages of Alchemy according to Ripley are Calcination and Solution. The first is described as "the reduction of the matters used to a non-metallic condition" (usually by application of gentle, external, heat). In Richard Cavendish's interpretation of this process, he suggests, "Calcination probably stands for the purging fires of aspiration and self-discipline ... The work begins with a burning discontent with oneself and one's life ... Combined with a fierce determination to do better, the result is the disintegration of the natural self. The outer, surface aspects of the personality are burned away and what is left is the 'powder' of the inner man." He also equates this process to the tarot card of "The Day of Judgment," which when combined with its corresponding path on the diagram of the Tree of Life gives a constellation of guidance to the spiritual aspirant.

The Alchemical Garden

In this method we take a visualized journey and receive our Tarot in imagination. You should allow thirty minutes and be sat comfortably.

Close your eyes and visualize yourself dressed as an alchemist; imagine what you would wear to become an alchemist, working with the mysteries of nature, space and time. Perhaps you are robed like a magician, garbed as a chemist, dressed as an artist, or a worker of metals. Feel what it feels like to be dressed in this manner. Now visualize yourself creating another version of yourself, stood before you, facing ahead (so you can see this figure's back). Imagine that as an alchemist you can create a slightly better image of yourself, perhaps only different in one slight detail, but making yourself a stronger image, nonetheless. See how this figure stands, holds their head, moves slightly. When you are ready to take a deep breath, step forward and 'stand into' that new figure, immediately feeling what it feels like, seeing out through their eyes, hearing with their eyes.

Now look forwards in your imagination and create another figure - an even more transformed version of yourself, using your slightly improved skills as an alchemist. Perhaps this next version is even richer in detail, more confident, maybe they are even surrounded by flames or a shimmer of light.

Make the image as powerful as you now can and when ready, taking a deep breath, step forward and inhabit that even more improved version, looking out through their eyes and feeling now all the abilities you possess. You may wish to repeat this at least three or four times.

Use sound, taste and smell whilst you strengthen your image; you may taste the clear taste of peppermint, or hear chimes, or smell rich incense that makes you think of gold. Use all your senses!

When you are fully present in your transformed alchemical body you can visualize a portal in front of you with the word VITRIOL upon it:

VITRIOL

This is often taken as an acronym for *Visita Interiora Terrae Rectificando Invenies Occultum Lapidem*: 'Search the interior of the earth and by rectifying thou shalt find the hidden Stone'.

Step through this portal and find yourself in a beautifully ornate and designed garden, with neat hedges, rose-bushes, paths and trellises. This is the Alchemical Garden and will be your meeting-place in vision and dream with the alchemical archetypes. Wander through the garden noting any details; perhaps there are statues, fountains, streams and bridges.

At last come to a central area, a cobbled square, perhaps, or other square space. Some people find themselves on a lawn, or an enclosed part of a hedge-maze.

Call upon the figure of **Salt** to present themselves to you with this suggested verse:

Open the Kingdom of Matter,

And come forth, O Sal

That I may know thy secret

And work to Higher Things.

Ask the figure: How may I transform my body?

Which Tarot card(s) do they show you?

Then call upon the figure of **Mercury** to present themselves to you. Suggested verse:

Many-eyed Mercurius,

Volatile and Quick,

Present yourself to me

That the medicine is created.

Ask the figure: How may I transform my mind?

Which Tarot card(s) do they show you?

Finally call upon the figure of **Sulpher** to present themselves to you. Suggested verse:

Separate the venom,

Sulpher, Oil and Fire

Be Quick to come

And fast to answer.

Ask the figure: How may I transform my emotions?

Which Tarot card(s) do they show you?

Then thank the figures for presenting themselves and gently return in your visualization to your stating point and open your eyes.

Recommended Reading

Stanislas Klossowski de Rola, *The Golden Game* (London: Thames & Hudson, 1988)

S. J. Linden, *The Alchemy Reader* (Cambridge: Cambridge University Press, 2003)

THE IAO METHOD

A Method designed to avoid stagnation and promote change.

There are certain magical formulae which describe fundamental patterns in the Universe, which can be seen arising in every manifestation, whether it be a multi-million-dollar building project or the play of children in a swimming pool. These formulae are used by magicians in initiation, in ritual, as shorthand and contemplative devices. They are used to effect change in the world. In this method we use Tarot keyed to a magical formula to resolve a "stuck" situation.

It uses the formula of IAO, which is an acronym of the translations of the hieroglyphs for the Ancient Egyptian Deities, Isis, Apophis, Osiris. This is described by Aleister Crowley:

> But before entering into the details of "I.A.O." as a magick formula it should be remarked that it is essentially the formula of Yoga or meditation, in fact, of elementary mysticism in all its branches.
>
> In beginning a meditation practice, there is always a quiet pleasure, a gentle natural growth; one takes a lively interest in the work; it seems easy; one is quite pleased to have started. This stage represents Isis. Sooner or later it is succeeded by depression - the Dark Night of the Soul, an infinite weariness and detestation of the work. The simplest and easiest acts become almost impossible to perform. Such impotence fills the mind with apprehension and despair. The intensity of this loathing can hardly be understood by any person who has not experienced it. This is the period of Apophis.

It is followed by the arising not of Isis, but of Osiris. The ancient condition is not restored, but a new and superior condition is created, a condition only rendered possible by the process of death.

The Alchemists themselves taught this same truth. The first matter of the work was base and primitive, though "natural". After passing through various stages the "black dragon" appeared; but from this arose the pure and perfect gold.

Take the following three cards from the Majors:

- Hermit (Isis as the Virgin, source)
- Death (Apophis as destroyer, transformer)
- Hierophant (Osiris as arisen sacrifice, interface)

Lay them out as follows:

Illus. Images from Silver Era Tarot (Kahn & Moon, Schiffer, used with permission)

Now shuffle the rest of the deck whilst considering your stuck situation.

Lay out three cards underneath the IAO cards above.

Read these cards as follows:

- **Hermit** position (I) – Where can I go to find my original inspiration?

- **Death** position (A) – What needs to change and be transformed?

- **Hierophant** position (O) – What will come after transformation?

You can lay a further row of cards underneath the IAO cards to further answer these three fundamental questions. You might also experiment with leaving the cards out for a few days to promote the change desired.

NAME SPREAD METHOD

A Method of turning a name into a **Spread**

There are many forms of numerology and ways of corresponding the English alphabet into numbers. We present here our own method.

A	1	J	10	S	19
B	2	K	11	T	20
C	3	L	12	U	21
D	4	M	13	V	22 (22)/Earth
E	5	N	14	W	23 (12)/Water
F	6	O	15	X	24 (0)/Air
G	7	P	16	Y	25 (20)/Fire
H	8	Q	17	Z	26 (0) Fool
I	9	R	18		

Using the table above you can convert any name into a spread and read the spread for the life of that person, with the four elements and Tarot.

MARCUS

13 + 1 + 18 + 3 + 21 + 19

Death + Magician + Moon + Empress + World + Sun

KATZ

11 + 1 + 20 + 26

Justice + Magician + Last Judgment + Fool

Last Judgment + Magician + Hanged Man + Hermit

Chariot + Devil + Devil + Emperor + WATER + Hermit + Temperance

Finding Amber Method (Tarot Shaman)

A Shamanistic Style Tarot Walk.

This next method is modified from our Spellcrafting Course which we teach at Magicka School (www.magickaschool.com). I am betting you will have never heard of it, as I have never seen anything like it published. It was taught to me almost thirty years ago by a Tasmanian Magician who was a font of pure magick. It is inspired in part by the *Chronicles of Amber* series of books by the fantasy author, Roger Zelzany, written starting in 1970. In this sequence of books, he depicts a universe of many worlds, connected by gates. The Princes of Amber – an idyllic world in the center of the multiverse - can travel through these gates. They come and visit our mundane world and a character asks them how they find their way back to Amber, as there are no obvious signposts or astral gateways or similar devices.

The Prince responds that it is very easy for him to find Amber, having known Amber. No matter where he is, he looks around him. Something he sees will simply be "closer" to Amber and its nature than other things. It could be a pattern on a leaf, a road sign, a person talking with laughter in their voice or an old wooden door in a room. He then makes his way to this object, and from there, looks again and repeats the process. As he then says, 'the final step to Amber is only ever at most about three or four objects away'. It is a process that is hidden in plain sight, like all pure magick.

So, our "Amber" is going to be the heart of one of the Major Tarot cards. We are going to spend a few hours or even a whole day working with this card in a unique fashion. First spend a moment thinking about the card on a literal level. What is it called? What does it show? Then think about the symbols on the card. What do they mean?

Then begin to extend the card. What does it remind you of? What places and people? What feelings? Now when you have connected to these levels of the card, look around you, wherever you have chosen to do this – it does not really matter if at home or away, inside or outside. Everywhere in the Universe is equidistant and happening at the same time – and in that manner connected - from a magical perspective, so let us start acting as if we know that all the time, particularly when we make magick.

What connects most to that card from right where you are sitting or standing now? What is closest to those feelings of the card, the symbols — even a literal object on the card?

Now go to that object, person or place. Who knows, something else might come to mind, a person you have not visited for a while, a place you only saw yesterday. Our magick ranges all time and space — do not be constrained. Then, when you are there, look around again — what seems closest again to your sense of the card? What draws you, what feels just so, what feels right? Then go to it. Repeat this a few times until you find yourself with something that feels like it is a gift to you from the card itself - an object that you can purchase, buy, pick up, take freely, or otherwise return to your home.

This object could be anything, but it will be what is called in Fluid Dynamics Sciences a "strange attractor" — and what in Magick is called a "vortex". Something that functions as a center of gravity, and about which everything else moves. This is now a magical Talisman of that card and can be used in further Tarosophy spellcrafting.

Pandora's Box Shuffle System

A Method of shuffling and selecting for questions where the Querent seeks hope.

"But the woman took off the great lid of the jar with her hands and scattered, all these and her thought caused sorrow and mischief to men. Only Hope remained there in an unbreakable home within under the rim of the great jar, and did not fly out at the door; for ere that, the lid of the jar stopped her, by the will of Aegis-holding Zeus who gathers the clouds. But the rest, countless plagues, wander amongst men; for earth is full of evils, and the sea is full. Of themselves diseases come upon men continually by day and by night, bringing mischief to mortals silently; for wise Zeus took away speech from them."

Hesiod, Works & Days

A Querent often arrives at a divination session and expresses a totally hopeless situation. They seek a divination which will give them such hope – hope that a situation will change for the better, is not as bad as they think, or will somehow turn positive.

Whilst it is not the Work of the Oracle to provide hope if none is to be discovered in the interpretation of the reading, unless they subscribe to such method, we can at the very least look for where hope may be discovered in life. In this method we simply add a little *twist* to our shuffle.

Take out the STAR card. Inform the Querent that this is a card which signifies vision, clarity and hope. Tell them if you wish about the card, the symbols and their meanings. Ask the client to hold that card for a moment. If you wish, you can ask them to describe what they see in the card. Allow such descriptions to be heard and recognized without judgment.

Then ask the Querent to insert the HOPE CARD into the deck.

Now ask the Querent to shuffle the deck whilst considering their hopeless situation, or the situation in which they are looking to discover change.

Turn the deck up and look through the cards until you discover the
STAR/HOPE card. Then on noting that you have found the HOPE card,
you can lay out your regular spread from the cards following the STAR.

You can also make 22 variants of this method by using the 22 Majors as
start significations of other usual contexts of questions, such as:

- Magician: A question where the Querent requires willpower.

- Lovers: A relationship question.

- Hierophant: A spiritual question.

- Tower: A question where the Querent is dealing with shock.

- World: When the Querent has no particular question.

And so forth. These Divinatory Signification cards become the archetypal
significator of the spread, based on the field of the question.

THE DIG

A Method of Confessional Cards to reveal the archaeological layers of your soul.

In the work of Teilhard de Chardin, we find a curious yet profound combination of archeology and spiritual mysticism. De Chardin found a hymn to the Universe and saw our role as "communion through action", which is part of the philosophy of Tarosophy, "Tarot to engage life, not escape it".

In this method, we use the Tarot to represent three stories on Mysticism written by de Chardin, which he termed *histoires*.

In this method, we deal with the nature of the Western Esoteric Initiatory System (WEIS as we call it) as a "process of exhaustion" (see *THE MAGISTER*, a forthcoming series of 11 books on the WEIS) and use the Tarot to reveal the layers of our soul and the gap between it and divinity.

In one of de Chardin's *histoires* he expresses a mystical experience where he realizes that the gap between his awareness and the object being perceived (in this case, a *Pyx* in a church) is a separation "by the full extent and density of the years which still remained to me, to be lived and to be divinized".[6]

Shuffle your deck in the morning. Take out one card, leaving it face down.

At the end of the day, turn over the card and read it as a spiritual lesson. If that card were a mentor, what would it be inspiring you to do? As an example, if it were the 2 of Cups, it might be suggesting you make good agreements with others in your life. Review your day in the light of this lesson and *confess* to the card (in your journal) where you have not met its standard.

The following day select another card and do likewise. As the days progress, begin to wonder what the lesson or virtue is being expected of you through the card you have not yet seen.

---

[6] Telhard de Chardin, *Hymn of the Universe* (London: William Collins & Sons, 1965) p. 53.

When you can discern the lesson being taught and it is the same as when you interpret the card at the end of that day, you can complete the exercise.

Blind Man's Bluff Method

A method for using tag-cards without the counting system of the Golden Dawn.

Illus. A game of blind man's bluff, drawn in 1803.

The game of blind man's bluff has been enjoyed since 500 BC in Ancient China. In this method we use each card in a sequence to discover the next card to read in our spread. This is similar to the Golden Dawn method of *Opening the Key* (taught in our Diploma Tarot course) but without the correspondences and counting mechanism.

Like the game, this spread should be time-constrained, for example, for ten minutes.

Consider your question, shuffle the deck. Take the first card from the top of the deck and read that card. Put it back in the deck and shuffle again. Now find that card and take it out again – with the next card down from it, this has been tagged by the first card and is now read, becoming the *jīn dài* or "it" card. Take the first card out of play and put the second card back in the deck and repeat. Read the cards in sequence until the time is up. You can also use this method with Court Cards only for seeing how people will interact with each other or energies will flow in a situation.

Sing Song Method

A most unusual method where the Querent determines the time of the divination.

Do you prepare your Querent or ask them to prepare themselves for a divination? In ancient Delphi, postulants to the Oracle were placed through several preparatory situations, including bathing, fasting or being sent away to come back at a later and more propitious time.

In this method, we ask the Querent to call us for the reading only under a particular circumstance. We therefore need the Querent to have our contact number and we need to have a deck nearby at all times.

Ask the Querent to go away and only contact you when they hear a particular song or music, under any circumstances, or piece of dialogue, that reminds them of their situation or question.

They are then to immediately call you and you perform the reading over the phone at that moment – whether you provide them the details of the reading there and then or at a follow-up consultation.

This usually seems to result in telephone calls from shopping malls or restaurants but always adds to the divinatory moment. It also means that the Querent does not take the divination lightly and is involved in the mechanism of the reading on a far more subtle yet profound level.

Sun Meets Moon Spread

A 17-card spread for determining the conscious and unconscious aspects of a situation.

Lay out eight cards in a solar circle and nine cards in a lunar crescent along the lines of the template below.

Illus. Sun Meets Moon Layout.

Where the 3 cards of the Sun section meet the 3 cards of the Moon section, this is where the breakthrough in understanding can be made.

The Solar cards represent conscious factors in play, the Lunar cards represent unconscious patterns at work.

You can also use two decks for this method, one for the Solar cards and one for the Lunar cards, giving rise to the possibility of the same cards appearing in both aspects of the reading.

The Victoria's Secret Spread

A spread for divining the best course of action for a fight, or combative situation.

In this method, we take a Greek myth and create from it a spread. In fact, the myths of ancient Greece, Rome and Egypt are good places from which to derive spreads as the mythology was so specific to context, such as having a God for the Arts, a God for the Shepherds, a Goddess for Childbirth. If a client has a specific question in advance, you can prepare for the reading by discovering the appropriate myths for that situation and weaving them into your reading.

So, in this spread, we look at how to divine for a situation where there is argument and the Querent wishes to know how to act to get the best from the combative situation ahead.

As appropriate for a *Twist* reading, we add in a dash of magic by performing a brief invocation to the appropriate deity before commencing the reading, if we wish to gain divine favor.

Invocation of Victoria/Nike

Omnipotent Nike, desired by all

I invoke Thee –

Beat your wings against injustice!

Confer the battle trophy,

The Victors wreath,

The Mark of Sweet Renown.

Then perform the 4-card reading with the assistance of Styx's Children, including Nike, which are Nike (Victory), Bia (Force), Zelus (Rivalry) and Kratos (Strength).

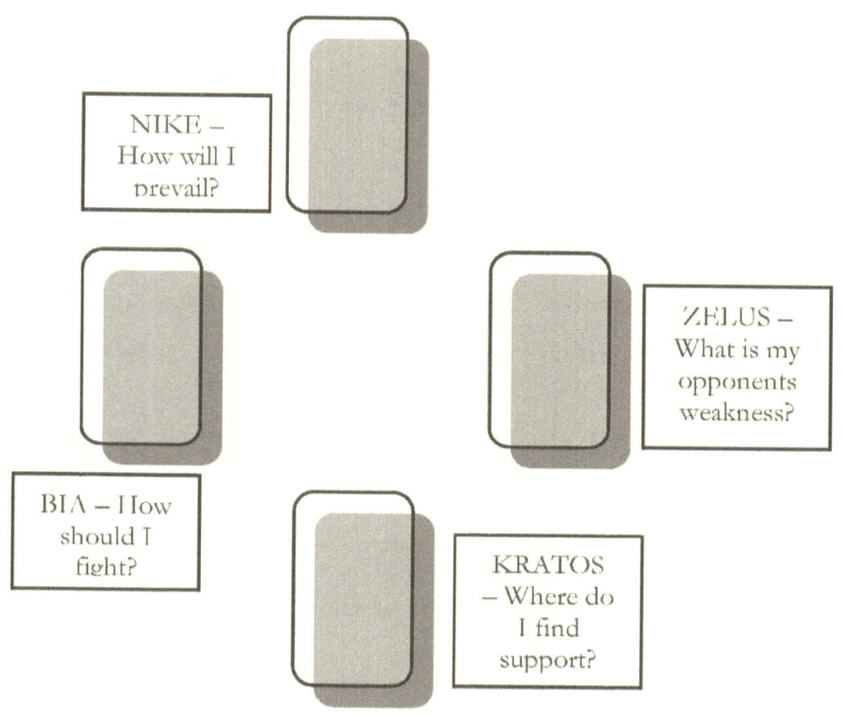

Illus. Victoria's Secret Spread.

House on the Borderlands Method

A means by which we use your dreaming soul to perform Tarot readings.

The unconscious mind works very much by conditioning and expectation setting. In this method we promote expectation and utilize our ability to dream. Recent studies have shown that eye-accessing in REM sleep reflects our dreamt activities, so we also use this phenomenon.

This process usually takes 1-2 weeks at most to gain a result. If you do not have a result within this time, take a break and repeat the method again at some later time.

On the first night, before sleep, consider your question (even if it is on behalf of a Querent) and say out loud, firmly, "This card is the answer to my question!" Then take a Tarot card out of your deck and place it up above your eye line so you must look up at it. Keep your head still, but move your eyes up, deliberately. Look at the card and then place it back in the deck and go to sleep.

Repeat this for at least 5-6 days. You can keep a note of the cards and keep a note of any dreams you may recall.

On the seventh night, hold the deck again, say in a loud distinct voice, "This card is the answer to my question!" and simply place the deck down and rest your head and go to sleep.

You may find that your unconscious, the moment your eyes look up during REM sleep, produces a Tarot card (or sometimes, a whole spread) in answer to your question.

My Mythic Story

A Method to write your life as a Mythic Story.

This method is given as one section in *The Garden of Creation*, which is a Tarosophy Gated Spreads. These Gated Spreads are week-long Tarot experiences comprising of usually 3-4 spreads or methods, linked by actions that must be taken between the spreads themselves. This is a unique way of working with Tarot in real-life and participants find the experiences life-changing.

In the Garden of Creation, we teach methods of using Tarot in creative writing, and this particular spread shows how to write a mythic narrative based on the universal archetypal story. Our *twist* is that it is a split-spread because different elements of the Tarot relate to different levels of the mono-myth.

1. Split your deck into three piles containing the Majors in one, the Minors in another and the Court Cards in the third. Shuffle each deck and lay them face down. Select cards from the appropriate pile as indicated below to create the cards for your story.

2. The first card, choose from the Court Card pile. This is the Hero(ine) and depicts his ordinary life. What sort of character is he (or she) and what sort of life does he lead?

3. The next card is a Major card and is the call to adventure. What changes in this person's life to start them on their journey?

4. The next card is a Minor card and is the nature of their refusal to go on this journey, engage with this event or opportunity. What do they do? How do they respond?

5. The next card, a Court Card (or you can select a Major Card) shows their Mentor. Who or What encourages them, teaches them, provokes them to change, and how?

6. The next card, a Minor, shows the first threshold that must be crossed, to enter a different world.

7. The next three cards (choose from any pile) indicates the tests, allies and enemies they encounter in this new situation.

8. The next card, a Major, shows the next threshold and the nature of the inmost cave — the secret heart of this story, a revelation, where they encounter the ordeal (select a Minor or Major card) and gain the reward (select a Minor or Major card).

9. They then take the road back to their starting-point (choose a Minor card) and cross a third threshold experiencing a transformation or resurrection. Finally, they return with a boon or elixir, a philosopher's stone and gift to bring to their previous situation. This is indicated by the final card, a Major.

This sequence is based on the mythic journey, or hero's journey described by Joseph Campbell and recast in contemporary style for authors, playwrights and screenwriters in Christopher Vogler's *The Writers Journey*.

We can utilize the cards in specific ways to creative dramatic narratives. These are seen in multiple aspects, where the Majors are archetypal forces at play, the Minors the events in everyday life manifesting those forces and acting as teachers, and the Court Cards personalities embodying these archetypal energies in mixed characters.

Whilst practicing creating these stories in this manner, you are also unconsciously learning ("installed") a new sense of how these cards represent these elements in a spread for a divination. You may find your ability to read cards progressively increasing and deepening as you practice these gates.

There is a universal story pattern which is the "Mono-myth" and all our lives partake of this mythic structure which is revealed in stories and any creative act. You may find that your garden plan and stepping-stones already reveal a lot about your own story.

A Note about Gated Spreads

You can discover more about Gated Spreads in our series of six books, given in the bibliography.

Recommended Reading

Christopher Vogler, *The Writers Journey* (London: Pan Books, 1999)

Joseph Campbell, *The Hero with a Thousand Faces* (London: Paladin, 1998)

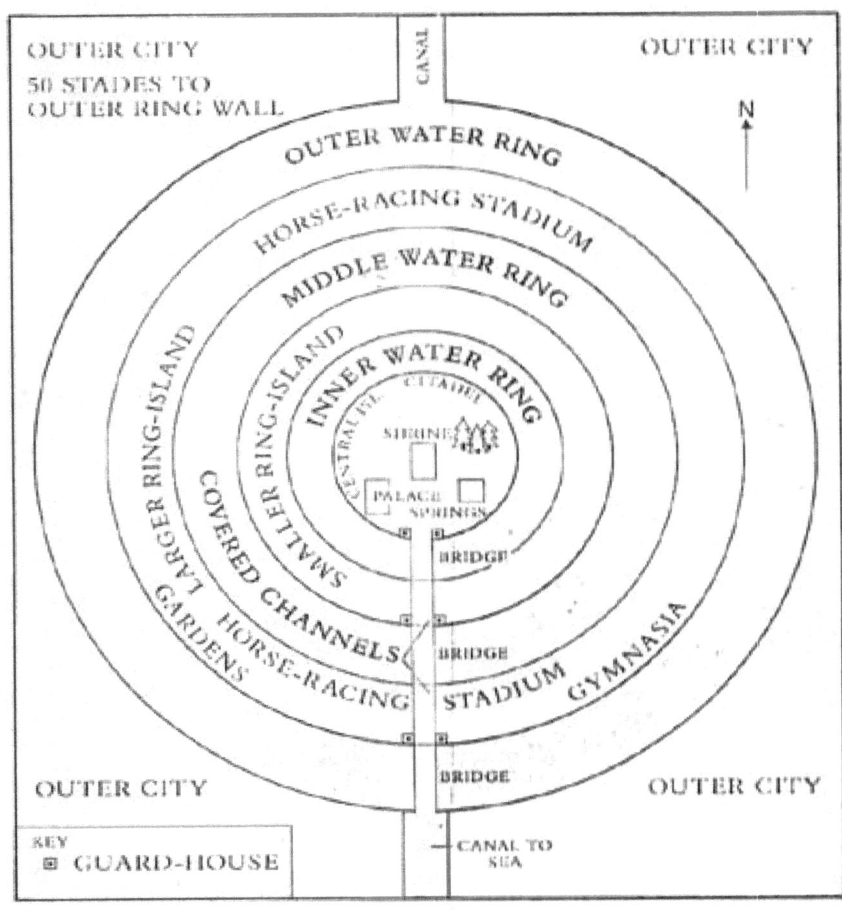

Rings of Atlantis Spread

An ancient method inspired by the mythic city of Atlantis and the Necronomicon.

Take 6 cards. Drop them in the bath or ocean. Wonder whether you should take anything seriously.

The so-called Lovecraft Variation: These cards will return when with strange Aeons even Death may Die. As it is said, *"Ph'nglui mglw'nafh Cthulhu R'lyeh wgah'nagl fhtagn"*.

Ancient Echoes Spread

An innovative method for discovering past-lives and their bearing on the present.

This is another split-spread method so first you will need to separate the Court Cards, Major Arcana and Minor Arcana into three stacks.

Take the Court Cards and shuffle. Lay out one card in the center of the table with the words "This is the nature of my Soul in present-time".

Take the Minor Cards and shuffle. Lay out two cards around the Soul card and say, "This is the nature of my lifetime in this life".

Once again, take the Court Cards and shuffle, looking at the two Minor cards. Take out one card and place it to one side (top/bottom, left/right) of the Minor cards and say, "This is an echo of my previous lifetime self".

Take the Major cards and shuffle. Select a card and lay it down between the two Court cards, saying "This is the Karmic lesson I must learn in this lifetime".

Take the Minor cards again and shuffle, considering the Major card of the Karmic lesson. Select out two cards and place them against the previous life Court Card, saying "This was the nature of that previous life". Weave a story from those cards.

You can keep repeating this method, by laying out another Karmic Lesson Major Card for the previous life Court Card and working outwards in echoes through all previous lifetimes.

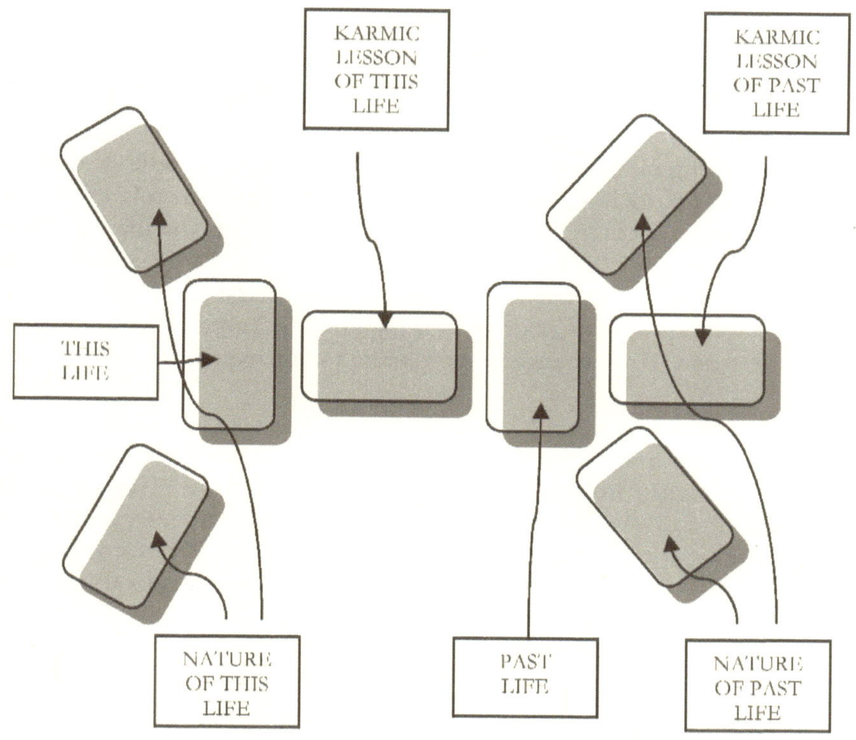

Illus. Ancient Echoes Layout.

You may choose to notice whether the previous life Minor cards are predominately male or female, particular suits denoting employment, and other such details.

You might also like to align your Karmic Lesson cards in a row and see if you discern any progression or pattern in those Major cards.

Candle Burning Method

A straightforward candle-magick spell souped-up with Tarot.

The following method is a special amalgamation of two methods we teach in the Magicka School 6-lesson Spellcrafting course.[7] In this exercise of spellcrafting, we demonstrate one of many ways which you may choose to use Tarot as a spellcrafting tool. Here we will use Tarot as a map and ritual to change a specific situation. We will be precise in the nature of the energy we require, using our own background in Tarot, to ensure that the manifestation of the change is appropriate to our requirements.

The Tarot cards depict the Universe manifesting itself in a variety of ways. This exercise introduces you to analyzing a situation you are currently living through, with the Tarot (and by implication the Tree of Life in Kabbalah) and then appropriately choosing a required energy to change the situation for the better, and using the appropriate Tarot card to invoke that energy in a gradual manner. This also provides a template for many other spells where you may require a gradual change rather than an overnight or abrupt change!

Follow the six steps below, having already defined your desire and moving into a state of neither-neither (meditation or dance, music, etc. prior to starting the exercise).

1. Take a situation you currently wish to change. What would you like to happen? Write this clearly on a piece of paper. You may also create a *sigil.*

2. What is the nature of the change that is required, in terms of the four elements and their corresponding Tarot Suit?

- Material change, money, finances, health … Earth/Pentacles

- Emotional, Fluid, Deep … Water/Cups

---

[7] www.magickaschool.com

- Intellect, Learning, Education … Air/Swords

- Beliefs, Lifestyle change, goals … Fire/Wands

Make a note of this Suit (Aspect to be Purified).

3. How far has the situation you are in got to? How long has it been going on?

On a scale of 1-10, where 1 is "I've only just realized I need to change something that has just started," to 10 "It's been going on forever and I'll never change it."

Make a note of this number (Developmental Stage to be Consecrated)

4. What type of energy is required to change the situation? Choose the appropriate energy from below which is given with the corresponding Court Card symbolizing that energy.

- Sudden, dramatic, fresh energy … Page

- Forceful, dynamic, piercing energy … Knight

- Stable, comforting, enduring energy … Queen

- Constant, fixed, robust energy … King

Make a note of the Court Card (Energy to be Invoked).

5. Now take a Tarot deck and select the appropriate MINOR card comprising the purification number (from step 3) and consecration aspect (from step 2).

For example, you would select the 4 of Pentacles, if it is a wealth situation (Pentacles) that has been going on a while but hasn't yet stabilized (i.e. 4 on a scale of 1- 10).

Also select the appropriate COURT card for the energy to be invoked (from step 4) in the same Suit (as step 2).

For example, the Page of Pentacles if you need a new fresh energy to break the wealth doldrums!

6. To carry out this spell-crafting, over a period of one week, begin by placing the MINOR card to the left of the COURT card somewhere convenient, i.e. where you can leave them and work with them for a week.

Leave a gap between them representing 7 card-widths. As each day passes for a week, move the COURT card one position to the LEFT towards the MINOR card.

This begins to bring the required energy into your life to change the situation, until on the last of the seven days, place the COURT card ON TOP OF the MINOR card which concludes and closes the spell. You may choose to leave the cards together for a further day and night to consolidate the spell. Then return the cards to your deck.

You can obviously amend this spell to work over a longer period of time (mark off smaller intervals and move the card a smaller amount) but it is recommended that you use a week or lunar month cycle at the minimum to ensure a graduated change.

There are other variations of this spell or you can use your imagination (i.e. working with all Four Suits in a Cross surrounding the Central Minor card and moving all four cards in towards the centre every day).

I have used this spell method on many occasions and found it subtle and effective. It also provides a hidden template for group temple workings where participants invoke appropriate forces and move in a brief ritual which reflects the cards, consecrating a Talisman in the centre.

We can add a Candle Magick spell at the same time as moving the cards together. Unlike most "candle magick" this uses two candles to ensure equilibrating forces (see also the "Path of the Seasons" article on "Uninvited Guests" in the *Magicka Magical Light Magazine*, July 2009).

Select an emotional state you wish to obtain whilst carrying out the Tarot spell, for example, "peace in turmoil", "confidence", "rest from anxiety". Using correspondences choose an appropriate color, i.e. blue for tranquility. Now, using a color wheel, find the complementary (opposite) color. So, for blue, we would select orange.

You can also purchase candles specifically designed for Tarot spells.

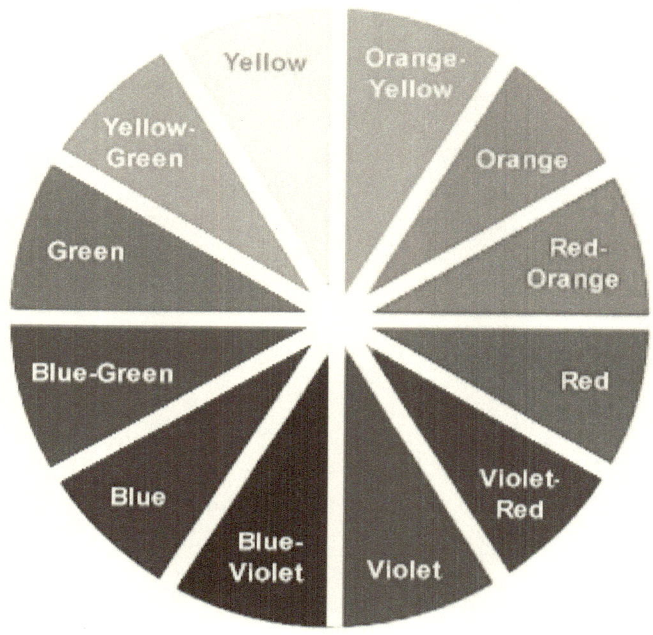

Now, purchase two candles, one of the state-color (e.g. blue) and one of the complementary colors (e.g. orange). Place these by your bedside (with the usual and common-sense safety observations) or on your altar, next to each other.

Every morning, spend 5-10 minutes and follow the ritual below:

1.   Light the State-Candle.

2.   Say "Not Now, but Later, I will feel even more [state]".

3.   Spend a few minutes noticing wherever you do not feel [state].

4.   Light the Complementary-Candle.

5.   Say "Spirit of the Opposition, I Bind You to [state]".

6.   Spend a few minutes noticing how the two candles burn.

7.   When ready to start the day, blow out both.

8.   Say "I have forgotten that which I did not need".

Record in your journal any noticeable changes in your internal state and external behavior as you conduct this spell over a week or lunar cycle.

Synchronicities Method

A Method using Tarot to promote synchronicity in life as a spiritual experience.

Plaskett's coincidence experiences alerted him in particular to the meaning of symbols: as he says, their conspicuously symbolic content "increased the attention I was giving to symbols." An eleven-page appendix to his narrative reproduces extensive extracts from various writings either showing symbolism in action (for example, in the spiritually orientated psychotherapeutic context of psychosynthesis), or discussing the nature of symbolism generally ... One thought occurring to him was that "in the light of such coincidences it seemed reasonable to postulate that some symbols have a power and significance wholly independent of the human mind".

Roderick Main, *Revelations of Chance: Synchronicity as Spiritual Experience*, p. 101

The practice of magical ritual often leads to synchronicities manifesting themselves in daily life. In fact, an immersion in magical thinking generates many such events until ultimately all life is seen as one continual synchronous event – a unified meaningful experience.

The practice of Tarot goes some way to promoting and experiencing this magical worldview, where the universe is "bound by invisible knots" or the "Web of Wyrd". In each reading we connect to the mysterious story of unseen patterns and processes of which we are the result.

To encourage this perception of synchronicity, a simple method may be undertaken. Take your deck and shuffle it until you feel the right moment to stop. Take out the top three cards and then look at the symbols contained in them, for example, a red cloak, a golden crown and a lantern.

The following day look for these symbols in your daily life – it could be a passing stranger in fancy dress, a pub symbol or a brand logo on a television advertisement. When you have seen one of these symbols in your environment, try it with just two cards, and then one.

You may be surprised how the Universe is interconnected and your part in its very creation.

PANDORA'S BOX SPREAD

"For Situations where there appears no hope"

Ask the Querent to contemplate the STAR card & consider "Hope".

Shuffle deck whilst Querent thinks of their Situation.
Give DECK to Querent. Ask them to look through deck for the 'HOPE CARD' (STAR).
When found, read the 1-3 cards prior to it as 'the last stages' and the 1-3 following cards as 'how you will locate hope'.

Sing Song Method of Divination by Tarot.

Tell the Client (or do yourself) that they should call you at only the moment they hear a song or piece of music that reflects their state or question. As soon as they call (or you hear the music) you do the reading!

N.b.

IMPORTANT You HAVE A DECK WITH You AT ALL TIMES !!!

YELLOW BRICK ROAD SPREAD
(Example of a 'Pulled Spread')

Take Significator, "This is Dorothy" Place in Centre of Table.
Shuffle deck, lay out 3 cards:

    ☐ LION   Ask Client (or Self)
    ☐ DOROTHY   "Which way to OZ?"
 ☐ ☐   Go with Lion, Tin Man
SCARECROW   TIN MAN   or Scarecrow!

Lay one card next to That one. "This is what will happen"
Lay a card against other two characters. "This is what pulls you". Ask again, "which way to OZ?" and repeat.

EXPLORE DEEPER ?
LION = WILL / COURAGE
TIN MAN = MIND / THOUGHT
SCARECROW = HEART / EMOTIONS

Useful for asking about a "Stuck" Situation

See P.78 'What To Do When You Don't Know What to do' (Neil Eskelin)

"VICTORIA'S SECRET" SPREAD
(Lol!) — For a fight ahead!

Invoke Victoria / Nike:

"omnipotent Nike, desired by all, I invoke Thee — Beat your wings against injustice. Confer the battle trophy, The Victor's wreath, the Mark of Sweet renown."
(see 'Hymns of Orpheus', R.C. Hogart)

Call Styx's children:

☐ NIKE (victory — how will I prevail?)

BIA ☐   ☐ ZELOS
(Force —   (Rivalry — what is
how should   my opponents
I fight?) ☐   weakness?)
KRATOS
(Strength — where do I find support?)

Illus. Creating and Using Spreads.

See no Evil, Hear no Evil, Speak no Evil (3 Monkeys Spread)

An immediately classic spread, the 3 Monkeys method uses NLP and Tarot.

We would like to thank Bernie Rowen and Nadine Roberts for assisting in the development of the Classic Three Monkeys Method during an online workshop for the Tarosophy Tarot Diploma course, mentored by Janine Worthington.

This method works well for highly personal questions or when reading for oneself. Shuffle the deck and take out nine cards. Place them in three stacks, face-down. These are the three monkey piles.

SEE NO EVIL   HEAR NO EVIL   SPEAK NO EVIL

Then ask yourself (or your Querent) when you consider your situation or question, is it something you see in your mind, in visualization? Is it something you hear, the sounds of someone's voice for example, or music? Or is it something you describe to yourself in words as an internal dialogue?

Whichever of those internal representations is foremost dictates which Monkey pile you pick. For visualized situations, pick See No Evil, for auditory situations, pick Hear No Evil, and for internal dialogue, pick Speak No Evil.

Then read the three cards as what you or your Querent is NOT seeing, hearing or telling yourself – and which you need to see, hear or be told.

Pit and Pendulum Method

Perfect for prediction of passage from peril and predicament.

In this method, mayhaps considered a parody of Poe, we look at a way of reading cards for when the Querent or oneself feels assailed by enemies and generally up against the wall.

Take your dire situation, particularly one with a deadline approaching.

Take out a Significator. Place it in the center of the table.

Shuffle the deck. Split it into two, face-down.

Take one card from the bottom of both piles and place the two cards in the center of the table next to each other, either side of the Significator. These are the RATS.

Now take another card from the top of both piles. Lay these out face-down at the top-end of your table furthest away from you. These are the PIT cards.

Now take the two piles and spread them out in two lines left and right of you. Begin to slide them in towards your Significator. These are the RED HOT WALLS.

When you feel that the situation is totally messed up on the table, with cards all over the place, take out the PIT cards and the RATS cards.

Read the PIT cards as divining the situation which is only feared but not really present and the RATS cards as an element in the situation you can use to escape, even if it means facing a fear.

The cards of the two walls are merely for dramatic effect.

This method can also benefit from the use of a pendulum.

In Two Minds Spread

A Method for performing a spread when you are in two minds about a situation.

In this split-spread, we use only the 14 cards of the Swords suit and the 22 Major Arcana. This gives you 36 cards.

Shuffle and decide on two positions, left and right, for the two sides of your decision, i.e. Stay or Go, Fred or Bill, Sell or Keep …

Lay out 6 cards in each "mind".

The cards indicate the nature of each situation as it will transpire.

The Majors in either row are the deciding factors and should be given due attention to the overall reading.

Second Opinion Method

A trick to get a second-opinion on your reading for yourself.

When you are reading for yourself, it can be difficult to perform a critical interpretation. One method is to place the cards down on a table as if you were reading for someone on the other side, then go and sit on the other side of the table and read them from that position, using the second-person language "You ..." and speaking out loud.

Another interesting way of getting a second-opinion, at a set financial cost to yourself (other than asking another reader to do it) is to simply take a clear photo of the cards and place them up as an advertisement in a shop some distance from you, with just your telephone number on the advert.

The advert should read, say for example, if you have a $50 budget for the reading:

REWARD! Can someone tell me what these are, and what they might mean? I think they are Tarot. Phone xxx-xxxx-xxxx and let me know what they mean if you know. Possible $50 reward for first helpful answer.

Golden Dawn Temple Spread

A spread to divine where healing may be found in the midst of sickness or suffering.

I come in the power of the light,

I come in the light of wisdom,

I come in the Mercy of the Light

The Light hath healing in its wings

> Neophyte Ritual, Hermetic Order of the Golden Dawn

In this spread, we take the layout and structure of the Neophyte ritual of the Golden Dawn, itself laid out to a synthetic ground-plan of Kabbalistic, Astrological and Tarot associations.

This spread is particularly suitable to devise a healing ritual upon, as the positions of the cards relate to so many equilibrated forces. The *twist* is that you can take the cards and place them around you or your sleeping area in the same positions (you in center of two triangles) for a short time to equilibrate your own environment.

These positions have the following signification:

- **Hierophant**: What is being revealed by this suffering.

- **Hierus**: "I am called fortitude by the unhappy" – where rest can be found.

- **Hegemon**: The reconciler between light and darkness – how this disease will be reconciled with life.

- **Stolistes**: The Water of the suffering – what is being emotionally refined within the sickness and pain.

- **Dadouchos**: The Fire of the suffering – what is being consecrated and refined through this time.

- **Kerux**: The Guide – where this pain will lead.

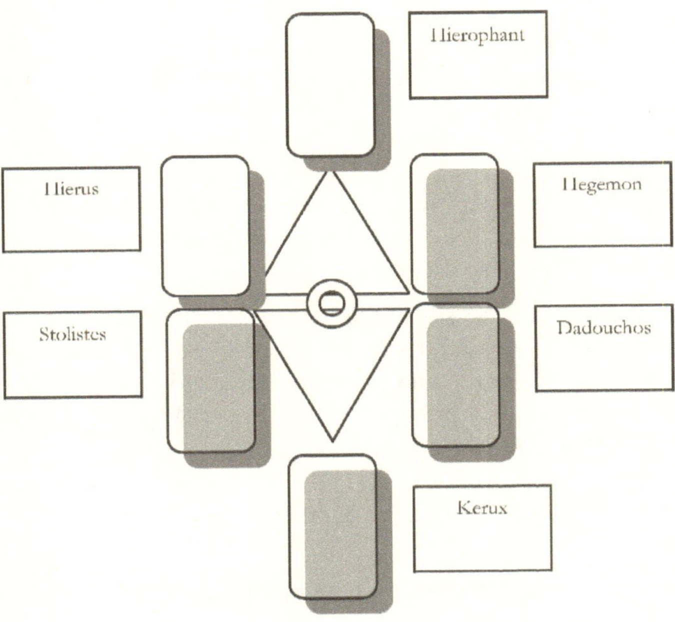

Illus. Golden Dawn Temple Spread.

Rose Cross Spread

A simple Rosicrucian Spread for spiritual wisdom.

This simple spread uses the word ROSA meaning Rose as an Acronym for the Spread meanings. This is a great way to design many spreads. It uses four cards which should be laid out in a circle.

Illus. Dat Rosa Mel Apibus.

Rose: What is unfolding in my spiritual life?

Occult: What is the secret of my hidden life?

Spirit: What is the spiritual path for me?

Action: What action will further my spiritual path?

Tao Tarot Method

A contemplative arrangement of the cards to reflect the Way of Water.

Take the Tarot deck and spread it out before you face-up. Begin to swirl the cards about with your hands, watching how certain cards move about, noticing how your eyes are brought to certain cards and colors. Notice how patterns form between the cards, but do not linger too long before they disappear again into the ever-present flow of movement.

Remember this swirling feeling when you next look at a flat still spread.

Your Spread

A challenge to you the dear reader.

When you read this page think of your own spread, from those inspired herein or the methods we have suggested at the end of this book. Have a look around you, see what inspires a spread, method or new pattern – a new way of using your Tarot.

This is the true purpose of this book, to ensure that you are free to develop your own approach to Tarot with your own distinct voice. Enjoy!

Toppling Pennies Spread (Push Method)

A Method for discovering where you can make a difference and divine the tipping point.

Malcolm Gladwell detailed much about the *Tipping Point* – the small things that make a difference, in his book of the same name. In NLP, we speak of the "difference that makes a difference". In Quantum Physics, there is a Catastrophe Theory which has also been utilized in Chaos Magick. In our lives at any given moment are threshold or liminal points where just one change can make a huge difference.

In this method we model how a threshold is created by a rather simple play on our cards, to divine where in our lives we should concentrate to make the biggest difference.

You need a large tabletop or similar raised smooth surface with an edge. Ensure that below the edge is nothing that will damage your Tarot cards other than a small drop. You can place something below the edge to catch your cards, or simply use a rugged deck.

Take your deck and consider all the opportunities you have, all the decisions you have made until this point. Consider how they tumble and fall into each other, like pushing the grains of sand across a vast beach of time ... now take your deck and face-down smooth it out across the table, mix it around, into a big circle of cards.

Then very gradually start to think about your future and push the cards as a mass towards the edge of the table. Think carefully about all the mistakes you have ever made, all the things that turned out differently than you expected. Allow some cards to start to fall off the edge of the table.

Then when you are content you have pushed the cards enough to represent your life thus far, select only those cards that are over the edge of the table but still hanging on in there – these are the tipping point cards and their interpretation will indicate where you can make differences in your life with most immediate effect.

For example, if my several tipping point cards were 2 of Cups, Devil, 3 of Pentacles and 3 of Swords, it would indicate a huge difference in my life would be created by working with somebody else in an exclusive manner.

Light /Dark Spread

A simple method to throw more light by less light on a reading.

Take a number of candles, with appropriate care and perform a standard spread with them lit and no other light source.

Extinguish one of the candles and notice how the images of the cards change, if at all, how colors become more significant, certain features become more or less prominent.

Extinguish another candle and repeat.

When all candles have been extinguished, spend 5 minutes in darkness seeing what you now notice about the spread in your mind.

The Night Train

A Visualization challenge when learning the Tarot or a new deck.

It should be possible for you to go to sleep whilst working through all the deck in your imagination.

Spend the time before sleep going through the Major Arcana in your mind's eye, seeing what you recall about each, and ensuring you can easily bring them to mind in the correct sequence.

Then see if you can work through each Suit, from Ace to Ten and then the Page to King in the Court cards. Perhaps practice with one suit for a week before moving onto the next suit.

You should be able to easily run through the entire deck in your mind in about ten minutes before sleep. This is a great experience to practice with a new deck and you will learn something new every night and every morning when you look at the deck again!

Sherlock Holmes Spread (Investigative Spread)

By eliminating the impossible in this method, we discover the improbable truth.

"You will not apply my precept," he said, shaking his head. "How often have I said to you that when you have eliminated the impossible, whatever remains, however improbable, must be the truth? We know that he did not come through the door, the window, or the chimney. We also know that he could not have been concealed in the room, as there is no concealment possible. When, then, did he come?"

Arthur Conan Doyle, *The Sign of the Four* (1890)

More often than not, Tarot readings are presented within a positive frame, that is to say, as a prediction of what will (or is, or was) happening. Here we *twist* that into a "not" frame, that is to say, what is **not** happening or likely to happen. We start at the absolutely **not**, and work inwards, so that whatever is **not** said, whatever remains, not matter however improbable, **must** be the truth.

In this method, we lay-out all cards face-down and then turn them all up at the same time, as in a dénouement at the end of a murder mystery. You will see throughout twist that sometimes cards are laid face-up, one at a time, or at the same time, sometimes laid face-down, and turned up one at a time. There are interesting differences in the way you go about reading in these various styles and it is worth investigating.

- Take your deck and shuffle.

- Consider the situation.

- Select one card. Lay it out face-down and say, "This is **not** happening".

- Lay out two cards beneath and say, "This is very unlikely the case".

- Lay out three cards beneath and say, "This is unlikely the case".

- Lay out four cards beneath and say, "This is probably **not** the case".

- Turn all seven cards up and investigate the matter.

Spread of the Ninth Arch (Typhonian Spread)

A dark grimoire spread to disperse nightmares of the nightside of the Tree of Life.

They say that Choronzon disperse; Set confuses; Chozzar dissolves; Yuggoth forgets ...

(The Book of the Spider: 8)[8]

The *typhonian* works of Kenneth Grant dwell upon the distinct differences between the rational conscious mind and the swirling voracious depths of the unconscious. When we have nightmares, this distinction is overwhelmed and the fears can play out in everyday life. If you are troubled by a particular concern, we can work with the dualistic "energies of the conscious mind", Choronzon, Set, Chozzar and Yuggoth, to absorb this fear.

This working is best done by candle-light and with a deck whose images disturb or challenge your sensibilities. The *twist* is that this is a spread that uses **only** reversed cards. Take your fear in your mind and heart and shuffle the deck.

- **Choronzon:** Lay out five cards face down. Turn them over with the words "This is what disperses my fear into the Abyss". Remove any upright cards. If all cards are upright, the reading is complete. Read any remaining reversed cards as advisory to the dispersion of your fear.

- **Set:** Lay out another five cards similarly, with the words, "This is what consigns my fear to darkness." Again, only read reversed cards. If all cards are upright, the reading is complete.

---

[8] Kenneth Grant, *The Ninth Arch* (London: Starfire, 2002) p. 12, p. 160

- **Chozzar**: Lay out five cards again, with the words, "This is how my fear is eaten". The same instructions as before apply.

- **Yuggoth**: Finally lay out five final cards, with the words, "This is how my fear will be forgotten". Here also, only reversed cards are read.

Dream Spread

Working with a Dream through Tarot.

In our Tarot workshops, we tend to teach a Jungian approach to dreams, with a reasonably standard interpretation of the environments, symbols, characters and events taking place within dreaming. As Tarot is based on images of the same archetypal energies as contacted within dreams, it is sensible to create a living dialogue through Tarot which teaches our mind to use this expressive language.

Take THE MOON Tarot card and look over it before sleep.

Imagine it in your mind as you go to sleep. You may find it helpful to imagine it moving slightly towards you when breathing in, and slightly away each time you breath out, so it gently floats in and out of your awareness. As you fall asleep, as best you can, feel as if you are falling into the card – make it bigger as it comes towards you until it surrounds you.

Record any dreams in the morning. You may continue this exercise with the same card until you have one or two dreams.

When you have a dream, consider it to be the basis of a situation about which you are performing a divination with your Tarot. We use a split-spread, so divide your deck into Majors, Minors and Court Cards.

The recognizable lead characters in the dream are known aspects of your conscious mind – for each of the characters in the dream pull one Court Card to divine its nature.

Any strangers in your dream are unknown parts of your self – for each pull one Court Card to divine its message to you.

The environment (house, playground, ocean, etc.) of the dream is your representation of your own character – pull three Major cards to divine its message.

The events in the dream are representations of unconscious processes and patterns – pull four cards from the forty Minors only to divine the message of these processes to you at this time.

ABRAHADABRA Method/Spread

A magical Tarot Triangle spread for removing oneself from an unwanted situation.

The magical phrase **Abracadabra** is written into our consciousness from an early age, particularly those of us who attended British pantomimes or have watched children's stage magicians.

The word of power is particularly useful as a means of ridding oneself of an unwanted situation, particularly where you wish someone would simply swallow their own words. By using Tarot, we can define, divine, and disassociate ourselves from the situation in one combined method.

Take consideration of the situation, shuffle the deck and lay out 11 cards in a straight line from left to right. These divine the situation as it presently exists. Leave the cards out for a day and night. On the second day, remove the last card from the right-hand side of the line. This now shows the situation being open to change.

ABRACADABRA
ABRACADABR
ABRACADAB
ABRACADA
ABRACAD
ABRACA
ABRAC
ABRA
ABR
AB
A

Illus. ABRAHADABRA.

On the third day, remove the next card, and so forth for a period of ten days until you are left with only one card, the card which was on the left of the whole spread. This is the card which frees you from the situation.

Remove that card and return it to the deck. If the magick works, the situation will resolve — at the very least, you will have gained more insight into the situation itself over the eleven days.

The Road Less Travelled (Unusual option spread)

A Method for divining out-of-the-box solutions to intractable problems.

For this method, it is recommended that you use a deck to which you are not commonly drawn, if at all. Find the most outlandish (in your opinion), horrible (to you), and unreadable (by you) deck possible.

Take four cards for your reading, having considered the problem.

Place the four cards in a tight box arrangement.

Then lay out the next twelve cards in a tight box around the first four.

Lay out the next twenty cards in another box around the previous ones.

Lay out a larger box of twenty-eight cards around the previous ones.

You should now have a box-grid of cards eight-by-eight.

You will be left with fourteen cards out of that box.

Put away the cards laid out on the table and lay out the first nine of the fourteen cards in a three-by-three box arrangement.

Discard those cards too.

The remaining five cards are the out-of-the-box solution to the problem.

A Note on Performance

You may realize that this method, like some, can be easily shortened – in this case by simply taking the last five cards out of the deck once shuffled. However, this is not the point. How we arrive at those cards – the journey we take – is as much part of the solution as the destination. You may also note certain patterns arising in the layouts before you discard them, particularly at the corner cards.

When performing this reading for a client, it is also part of the delivery to import the nature of the answer as being unexpected but appropriate.

My Secret Garden (Feminine Mysteries Working)

Discover the Way of Initiation for the Feminine.

The Tarot is a repository of sacred myth and story. It is the myth of the divine, the creation and of our daily life. At a certain level, it is gender-based, showing the projection of masculine and feminine qualities in its symbols and characters.

To explore this duality, work through your deck and take out all the cards which you would deem feminine. Leave any masculine cards or those of which you are unsure in the deck.

Take the feminine energy cards and shuffle them.

Lay out nine cards in a row.

See these cards as a narrative sequence, a Heroine's Journey. For men, this will explore your Anima.

Devise a daily routine over **nine** days and nights that reflect the energy and challenges of these nine cards. Ensure every day has a challenge or test devised upon the particular card, and a reward.

Now take out the "masculine" cards for **six** days and do the same. Consider them as a Hero's Journey – for women this experience will explore your Animus.

Compare and contrast the experience of the two sequences.

You might devise your experiences using the books listed below.

Recommended Reading

Maureen Murdock, *The Heroine's Journey* (Boston: Shamballa, 1990)

M. Esther Harding, *Women's Mysteries* (London: Century, 1999)

Sylvia Brinton Perera, *Descent to the Goddess* (Toronto: Inner City Books, 1981)

Strong Like Bull (Masculine Power Working)

Create a Tarot Dream Snare for powerful and precise dreaming.

Buffalo, Bison, Tatanka

With strength in your stride you grace the earth

In natural rhythm and harmony

You teach the cycle of abundance

And the selfless ability to give of ourselves.

In this method we create a powerful Dream Snare fashioned of the Tarot cards which will attract the vision and invoke the powerful spirit we require for a task in hand.

Take out of your deck the most powerful representation you can find of the spirit you wish to capture in your dreams, be it courage, intellect, wisdom, or love.

Place that card in the center of a table.

Place around it four cards which represent to you protective spirits, guardians or other means of defense and protection.

Now take the rest of the deck and shuffle it whilst concentrating on the five cards you have placed upon the table.

Draw six cards which represent the Upper World of which the five drawn previously are of the Lower World.

You can now fashion these cards into a *mandala*, perhaps by photographing them or otherwise working with them.

Hang this image above your bed for powerful dreams.

5 Stages of the Soul Spread

Using Tarot to locating yourself in the five stages of your souls journey.

The day you were born a ladder was set up to help you escape from this world.

Rumi

According to the work of Harry R. Moody and David Carroll, the soul passes through five distinct stages:

1. The Call

2. The Search

3. The Struggle

4. The Breakthrough

5. The Return

In this straightforward spread, we shuffle and select three cards for each line of the stages, answering the following questions:

1. To what do I need to heed to hear my very souls Call?

2. On the Outer and the Inner, what practice is my Quest?

3. What is the nature of the struggle that is my Way?

4. Where can I find Initiation?

5. What is my spiritual Task?

Recommended Reading

Harry R. Moody & David Carroll, *The Five Stages of the Soul* (London: Rider, 1998)

LOL Spread

A divination by humor, honoring the muse of comedy, Thalia.

Comedy, like divination, is a matter of timing. The Muse sacred to comedic matters is *Thalia*, the Muse who assists men to flourish when they are praised in poetry. The structure of a joke is much its own language as a Tarot reading, and here we use that structure to create a Tarot spread which reframes any situation.

The *twist* with this method is that it is an example of a *linked spread*, where (in this case) three different spreads relate to each other.

Take a situation where you would like to see things differently.

A. The Setup

First lay out three cards – the Protagonist [Card 1], and the Inciting Incidents [Cards 2 & 3]. These tell you of the character flaw which is being exposed by the situation and the way in which the world exposes that flaw.

B. The Dramatic Necessity

Now perform another reading, taking the cards back into the whole deck and shuffling again. Lay out five cards.

These tell you of the pattern by which this event will continue to play out until you get the punchline.

C. The Punchline

This spread is a re-framing all that has gone before. Take all the cards back again and shuffle. Then take the three cards at the bottom of the deck and these will tell you the lesson to be learnt from the event.

If the punchline does not make any sense to you, it is clear that you have not yet got the joke.

The Muses Spread

A spread for divining your creativity or a creative solution to a problem.

Hesiod even gives their [the Mousai] names when he writes: "Kleio, Euterpe, and Thaleia, Melpomene, Terpsikhore and Erato, and Polymnia, Ourania, Kalliope too, of them all the most comely." To each of the Mousai men assign her special aptitude for one of the branches of the liberal arts, such as poetry, song, pantomimic dancing, the round dance with music, the study of the stars, and the other liberal arts ... For the name of each Mousa, they say, men have found a reason appropriate to her: ... Thaleia, because men whose praises have been sung in poems flourish (thallein) through long periods of time.

Diodorus Siculus, Library of History 4. 7. 1 (trans. Oldfather) (Greek historian C1st B.C.)

Lay out three cards, one for each of the Muses. She will speak to you through those cards and inspire you.

Illus. A Muse.

- **Calliope**, the muse of epic poetry: these three cards inspire you to hear the poetry and structure of the situation.

- **Clio**, the muse of history: these three cards tell you all that has befallen previously in this situation.

- **Erato**, the muse of love poetry: these three cards will tell your heart what it seeks within the situation, and what rewards will come.

- **Euterpe**, the muse of lyric poetry: these three cards tell you of the song which is being sung, the message to your soul.

- **Melpomene**, the muse of tragedy: these three cards warn you of where to be careful.

- **Polyhymnia**, the muse of songs of praise to the gods: these three cards tell you how to act to ensure just reward.

- **Terpsichore**, the muse of choral songs and dance: these three cards show you the next actions to take to be creative.

- **Thalia**, the muse of comedy: These cards hint at what might be let go in the situation and what might be considered unimportant.

- **Urania**, the muse of astronomy: These three cards indicate the timing of the situation and its revelation.

The 4 Faces Method

A method working with the past and future of a relationship.

Janus also has a temple at Rome with double doors, which they call the gates of war; for the temple always stands open in time of war, but is closed when peace has come. The latter was a difficult matter, and it rarely happened, since the realm was always engaged in some war…

Plutarch, Life of King Numa 20.1-2

Nearly 3 in 5 questions you will ever be asked as a Tarot Reader will be regarding relationships. And whatever your beliefs and feelings may be about the concept of "soul mates" you had better be well-researched in that area and know your own opinion, as it is a phrase you will hear a lot.

In the Four Faces spread, we use the Court Cards and the Minor Cards only to work dynamically with a relationship situation, contemplating both its past and its future in the guise of Janus, the two-faced God who looked into both the past and future.

Shuffle the Court Cards only. Take out two cards face-up, place them several cards-widths distance from each other. These are the two people in relationship.

Take the Minors and shuffle. Place one card either side of the two Court cards, to show the past that each person is bringing to the relationship.

Place one card the other side of the two Court cards to show the future they are moving into through the relationship.

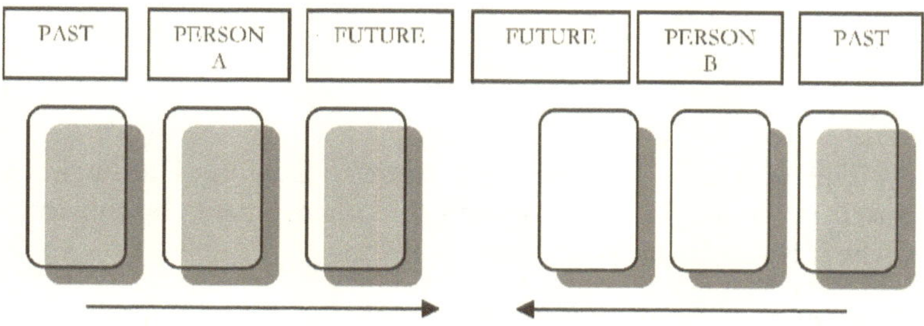

Egyptian Soul Spread

A Spread for looking at how the levels of your Soul are arrayed within a Karmic issue.

The ancient Egyptians created a vast architecture of the soul and its passage through the worlds. In the hieroglyphs they coded the nature and quality of twelve levels of the human being, each with its own distinct function and representation. In this spread we imagine that for some questions a Karmic issue is being worked out, and all levels of the soul should be consulted in its resolution.

This spread uses 12 cards, selected from a shuffled deck and arranged in a circle. The twelve positions (in the order you choose to place them) accord with the twelve layers of the soul as given in the table following.

Egyptian Name	Glyph	Qualities
Khat (Kat, Xat, Kab)	Fish	Body
Sahu	Mummy & Seal	Spiritual Body
Ka (Kai)	Upraised hands	Image, Double
Ba (Baie)	Various birds	Spirit-Soul
Khaibt	Fan	Shadow, Aura
Akh (Khu, Khou, Yekh)	Bennu bird	Bright Spirit
Sekhem	Owl	Vital Power
Ren	Kneeling man	Name
Hati	Lion	Whole Heart
Ab	Jar	Will
Tet (Zet)	Upright snake	Soul
Hammemit Radiating sun		Unborn Soul

1. Body: This card shows the physical nature of how my Karmic issue is manifesting in the world of action and the environment. It explains the reason why it is this situation and not another.

2. Spiritual Body. This card shows the spiritual aspect of the situation.

3. Image, Double: This card reflects how I have projected in my imagination the explanation of this situation.

4. Spirit-Soul: Moving up, this card now shows how my spirit-soul must make its transition through the situation.

5. Shadow, Aura: The card in this position shows the issue I am not facing – and must face – to resolve this Karmic knot.

6. Bright Spirit: This shows the positive nature of what can come out of facing this issue.

7. Vital Power: This card shows the resources upon which I should draw to overcome and resolve the Karmic debt or legacy.

8. Name: This is my own identity being formed by engaging with this experience.

9. Whole Heart: The emotional content of the situation – how it is being.

10. Will: The dynamic content of the situation – where it is going.

11. Soul: The sublime mystery above and beneath this passing moment.

12. Unborn Soul: What will be born out of myself in future.

Mistake Spread

A Spread to make the most of your mistakes.

When you make a mistake, whether it is a simple one, a complex one, or a lifetime one, it is sometimes difficult to move on from it. This next method uses our installed "parental voice" to ensure we have opportunity to move on from our mistakes, or work with a Querent to help them move onwards.

It uses a version of the Tarosophy Gated Spreads, which provoke action between a series of gated spreads for the whole reading/experience to unfold. This is a unique method, like most in this book, and can be extremely powerful.

It is a split-spread, so take out the Court Cards, Major Cards and Minor Cards in three different stacks. This method also uses **reversals**, so ensure you have cards both upright and reversed as you shuffle the stacks.

Take out two cards from the Minors and lay them next to each other. This represents the nature of your mistake. Spend one day considering this pair of cards – particularly if either or both are reversed.

The following day take out two Court Cards and place them above the mistake cards. These represent your parental or inner critical voice. Spend a day contemplating what that is telling you about the mistake.

The third day take a Major Card out and turn it up, and this will divine the action you can take to move on from the mistake.

Do not move on to the next part of this divination until you have taken that action – like the full Gated Spreads, this method is engaged with life.

When you have taken that action, you can now turn over a Major card which will indicate what you have now learnt from working with the mistake.

You can also *twist* the reading by adding two further Minor cards on top of the two representing the original mistake, to divine how you might now reframe that original action, and two Court Cards on top of the originals to divine the positive aspects of the original self-talk or critical voice.

The Alphabet of Desire Method

A method by which a card is opened for divination by the neither-neither state.

The trance and sigil work of Austin Osman Spare (1886 – 1956) is the inspiration for this method, which takes us deeply into the symbolic language of a card through visualization and automatic writing.

You will need a mirror for this exercise and a particular Tarot card, chosen by yourself for exploration or in answer to a question. You will need a large sheet (or many) of paper and a good pen.

Hold a pen in your dominant hand above the paper. Place the Tarot card in front of the mirror and gaze into the mirror at your own reflection. Keep doing so until you begin to go blurry and start to feel as if you don't recognize your own reflection. On occasion, gaze down at the card and see the colors of the card, contrasting with each other, and imagine that the colors are their opposites and beyond. Where you see red, imagine all that is not red.

You can begin a breathing pattern if you wish at this point, perhaps breathing 4-in, 4-out for a while, then 4-in, hold for 4, 4-out, hold for 4.

Start to see the colors flowing around the card as if they were fluid and running. Now look back at your reflection for a while, and then when you next look at the card, see the individual symbols of the card "coming lose", floating into the card, floating out of it. Attain a dream-like state.

Look back in the mirror one more time and then drop your eyes to the card and close them, feeling yourself fall into the card as if a dream. Let the colors swirl around you, the symbols float, like the scene in Wizard of Oz as Dorothy goes up the tornado.

Now begin to allow the symbols to arrange themselves as if they were characters in a film, letters and words in a sentence. Allow them to simplify themselves in primal forms, shapes, symbols, stick figures. Begin to draw as you will on the paper with your eyes remaining closed and relaxed. Breathe slowly and deeply throughout.

Whatever you feel willed to draw, draw. Maintain your mind on the symbols, the arising alphabet of desire. When the symbols begin to lose their shape or substance, you can begin to re-orientate to the room and your position until you are ready to open your eyes again.

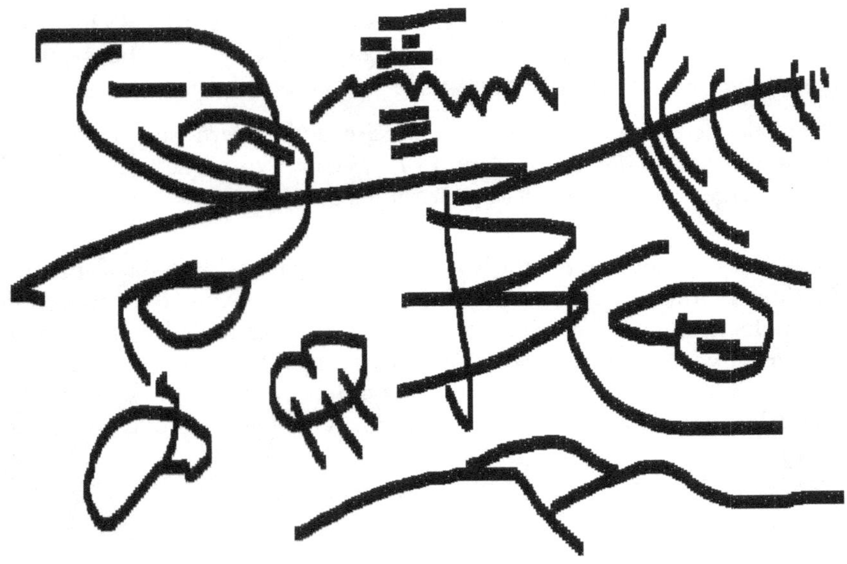

Illus. Free Sigil Drawing.

Contemplate the drawings for a moment before returning to everyday awareness and life. Do not then interpret the resulting symbols, sketches or scrawls. These are merely the detritus of the unconscious encounter. In the above example we might discern a face, a landscape, weather, a letter, even an I-Ching Hexagram. You can leave these for later.

For a few days, allow the sketch to be present whenever you are able, it will function as a sigil leading to sudden inspiration with regard to the question. There will be no doubt when this occurs, usually within a few days to a week. If there is no conscious and discernible result, you may dispose of the sketch in some short ritual (burying, burning, leaving to water or the elements) or paste it into a journal for later recollection.

Emerald Tablet Spread

An Alchemical and Hermetic spread

The Emerald Tablet is a hermetic text dating long prior to the 14th Century when it became a source for many alchemical works. It is a short piece of enigmatic verse detailing the "working of the sun". Yet despite its brevity, it is a profound text for contemplation and a worthy basis of a spread to explore the true nature of a situation.

Select out cards as appropriate to represent each verse of the text:

The Emerald Tablet Spread

[It is] true, without error, certain and most true,

[Card 1: What is the essence of this situation]

That which is below is as that which is above, and that which is above is as that which is below, to perform the miracles of the one thing.

[Card 2: How does the situation in the physical reflect the spiritual?]

And as all things were from the one, by means of the meditation of the one, thus all things were born from the one, by means of adaptation.

[Card 3: What is changing?]

Its father is the Sun, its mother is the Moon, the Wind carried it in its belly, its nurse is the earth.

[Card 4: What is nurturing the situation?]

The father of the whole world [or "of all of the initiates"?] is here.

Its power is whole if it has been turned into earth.

[Card 5: What action can be taken?]

You will separate the earth from the fire, the subtle from the dense, sweetly, with great skill.

[Card 6: What will bring peace to this situation?]

It ascends from earth into heaven and again it descends to the earth and receives the power of higher and of lower things.

[Card 7: Where can I receive assistance?]

Thus, you will have the Glory of the whole world.

Therefore, will all obscurity flee from you.

[Card 8: What do I need to know that is presently hidden?]

Of all strength this is true strength because it will conquer all that is subtle and penetrate all that is solid.

Thus, was the world created.

[Card 9: What is the Creative Act being undertaken?]

From this were wonderful adaptations, of which this is the means. Therefore, am I named Thrice-Great Hermes, having the three parts of the philosophy of the whole world.

It is finished, what I have said about the working[s] of the Sun.

[Card 10: How will I complete this situation?]

WARRIOR, SETTLER, NOMAD SPREAD

"How do I go about dealing with a tricky situation?"

* MINORS ONLY *

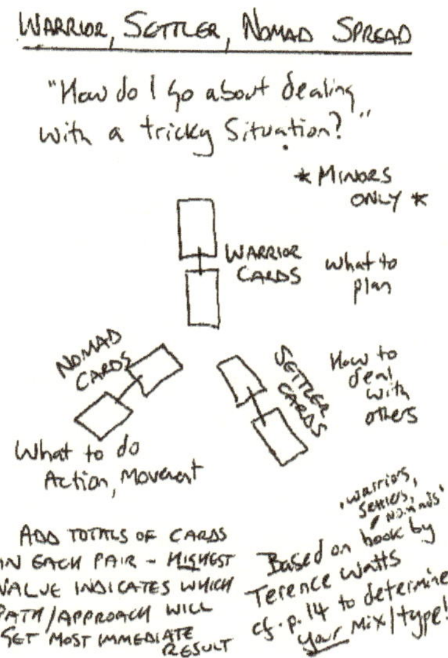

ADD TOTALS OF CARDS IN EACH PAIR — HIGHEST VALUE INDICATES WHICH PATH/APPROACH WILL GET MOST IMMEDIATE RESULT

THE YEAR LEFT TO LIVE SPREAD

* CAUTION! *
SERIOUS SELF-DISCOVERY LIKELY

Based on Stephen Levine's brilliant "A YEAR TO LIVE: HOW TO LIVE THIS YEAR AS IF IT WERE YOUR LAST."

Imagine you had received a precise prognosis of 1 year to live. Draw 12 cards:

JAN — What is my initial reaction?
FEB — How do I prepare for death?
MAR — How do I live & heal?
APR — How should I live each day?
MAY — How do I review my life?
JUNE — How do I offer service?
JULY — who dies?
AUG — what is beyond my death?
SEP — How do I leave my body + belongings?
OCT — what message do I leave behind?
NOV — what is change?
DEC — How do I die?

(Example months only — can also use these cards as card of the month)

DREAM SPREAD / METHOD

Use Unconscious "reflection setting" to access powerful intuitive resources!

Before sleep, get your deck, say "This is the ANSWER to my question" and pick a card. Sleep. Repeat EVERY NIGHT for 6-7 nights. On the 7th night, say "This is the answer..." but leave the deck FACE DOWN. You are likely to DREAM a Tarot card that night! That card (and the picked ones) will answer your question.

CLIMB INSIDE YOUR SPREAD!

Get a spread, say, 8-15 cards.
Do a Reading.

Get some small post-it notes. Write the names of your cards in the spread on the post-its — one on each note.

Go round your house + stick the post-its up in their relative positions (or close to them).

LIVE INSIDE THE SPREAD FOR A FEW DAYS — WHAT DO YOU SEE DIFFERENTLY?

Illus. Spread Notes from a Personal Tarot Journal.

Turning a Question into a Spread with Clean Language

Many of the spreads and methods here have been designed in real-time with particular Querents asking questions which have turned into a spread. A case in point was for the "Strange Attractors" or "Whirpool" method, which arose because a Querent presented a particular case. We cover this in our other books but provide a version here for reference.

He asked a question which was framed as "I have two options, both of which are possible, one probably more desirable than the other, but I could sort of do both, and they're both a little bit out of my hands." However, whilst he was asking the question, he was motioning with both hands in circular motions on the table. This was to express his own unconscious model of how the two situations were moving and placed relative to each other.

So, I suggested we use the "classic Whirlpool Method", where we first lay two cards down, in two positions on the table, to show the source of the two situations, their essential nature. We then placed a ring of three cards around each of those two source cards to show how that particular situation would ripple out. We then placed a ring of six cards around each ring to show the final results of how the two situations would develop.

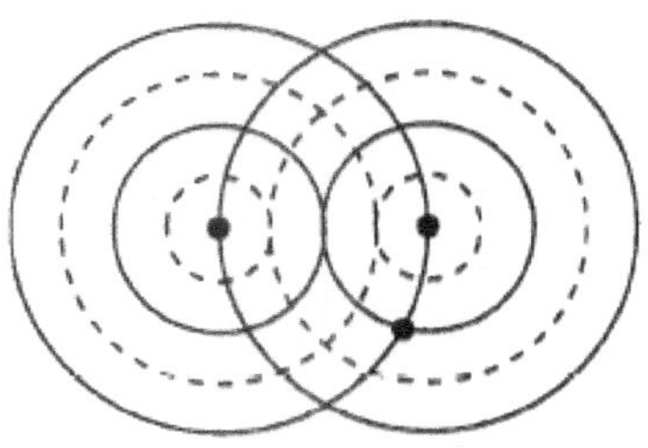

Illus. Whirlpool Spread.

However, by then, the two rings had expanded on the table to overlap each other, with two cards in particular touching each other from both situations. The Querent pointed these out and said, "I suppose this is what happens if I try to do both, they'll interfere with each other".

I nodded, and said, "so let's look at what happens in that case", and we laid out three cards around those two cards to show the interference pattern, like ripples on water. I now use this "classic" method whenever anyone presents a similar situation.

There is a simple method for learning this skill, which I have modified from the NLP-derived method of Clean Language, based on the work of the late David Grove, a therapist in New Zealand.

When someone expresses their question, it usually has an emotional content, and this can be turned into a metaphor by a specialized but straight-forward series of clean questions. It only takes a minute, and then you have a precise metaphor of the question against which to design your spread in real-time.

The sequence of questions is as follows, with the essential sequence highlighted in bold:

Querent: My question is X [including some emotional content, such as "and I'm concerned that I may not make the right choice"]

Reader: … and your concern. **Where is** your concern?

Querent: In my head [or Querent will gesture unconsciously even if they say "I don't really know"]

Reader: … in your head. **Is it outside or inside?**

Querent: Inside, in my head.

Reader: … inside, in your head. I'm wondering how you'd best **describe the shape or size** of that?

Querent: Well, it's just everywhere and it's rushing about.

Reader: … rushing about? **And that's like what?**

Querent: It's like a bull in a china shop, really.

So now you have a metaphor, the bull in a china shop. You can frame the questions in any particular way, following the Querent's own language.

The faster you do it, and the more you pay attention to their whole communication, including non-verbal gestures, the more noticeable it will be that the question suggests its own spread in response.

You can then apply the "Bull in the China Shop" as a reading method.

The Bull in a China Shop Spread

The Querent has asked whether to take an early retirement. They have described their question and given a metaphor which represents how their worries are rushing about like a bull in a china shop.

We take the symbols of **bull** and **china shop** to quickly lay out a reading.

1. The Bull cards. What is it that drives the client? [3 cards]

2. The China Shop card: What is it they will gain or lose from taking early retirement? [3 cards around the Bull cards]

3. The China Card: What will be broken by taking this step? [1 card]

Or any other variant that may strike you at the time of the reading, or as the Querent explains their question, or as the cards are laid down. In this approach, we are using our intermediate experience to be more responsive to the question in our divination rather than forcing it into a pre-determined spread. It also allows us to be more flexible and promotes an active dialogue with the deck and an engaging unique experience for the Querent.

Turning a Word into a Spread

If you are performing email readings, you can use a keyword in Querent's question to design an elegant and relevant spread. If a Querent has sent you this question, for example:

> Hello, I am asking about my relationship. I have been married for one year and we are discussing children. I wondered if I could have a reading because my parents used to say I was too **irresponsible** for such things and I am asking how my future might be with children.

Then we might take that word, irresponsible which I have highlighted above, as the main concern in the question. We then look up the etymology or derivation of the word in a dictionary or online source.

The word irresponsible comes from to be "not responsible". This in turn, "responsible" comes from a similar root ideas as "obligation". The word obligation comes from the Latin source, "to bind" and of course leads to its later use as meaning "to make someone indebted by conferring a benefit or kindness".

We take that concept, of debt and kindness, and turn it into the questions for a straightforward linear spread as follows.

The Parents Response Spread

1. What debt does the Querent owe her parents?

2. What kindness did the Querent learn from her parents?

3. What binds the Querent in their attitude to children?

4. What will the Querent be able to give beneficial to children?

5. What responsibility will the Querent take on?

6. What kindness will their child(ren) bring to them?

You can of course then riff out from those questions as the cards are placed, and engage in conversation with the spread itself. This can be a very powerful method because it takes much of the expectation of the reading out of your hands and places it from the Querents question directly in dialogue with the cards themselves.

Your job is simply to interpret the reading.

How to Have a Conversation with the Cards

Let the Cards Guide Your Spread.

An intermediate method of reading for a Querent is to simply allow the cards themselves to give you directions. This works in much the same way as stopping to ask people to give you directions when you are travelling. One person points you so far, then you have to stop again and ask another person from there!

So, when considering a question, simply read the first card on the top of the shuffled deck, then imagine how that card would guide you to the next card. If your first card was the Blasted Tower, you would read that as the first part of the spread, then perhaps suddenly drop all the cards and split them down the middle to select the next card.

If that next card were the Page of Wands, you might then wend your way through the deck picking one card after another until you got to a card that felt like your journey's end. If that card were the Ace of Cups, you'd read that card, then close your eyes and just let your feelings guide you to the next card. If that were the 10 of Pentacles, you'd probably just stop at that card as the final outcome of the reading.

Allowing the cards to direct you is a liberating experience and one of the first steps away from your beginner work into more dynamic and engaging work with the Tarot as your living guide.

Bonus Method 1: The Sign of Paracelsus

A method by which we engage with the signs of the world to direct our journey.

In the ninth book of the collected writings of Paracelsus, the Renaissance physician, alchemist, botanist and occultist, translated by A.E. Waite, Paracelsus writes on "the signature of natural things". He remarks that there are three signatories to the world; Man, *Archeus*, and the Stars of the Supernaturals. Whilst Adam was the first signatory of man, the *Archeus* being the lowest level of the Astral, it is the Stars which give "prophecies and presages".

In this method, we use the Tarot to direct us towards right action based on the presages of the cards relating to the astrological signs.

Take the following cards of the Majors:

- Sun
- High Priestess
- Blasted Tower
- Magician
- Wheel of Fortune
- Empress
- World

These correspond through their planetary correspondences to the days of the week, from Sunday (Sun) to Saturday (World). Shuffle the seven cards and select one. This will inform you which day of the week you are to look for a sign or portent in answer to your question. Do not consult the cards at any time until that day arrives, and then only consult the cards when the sign has been revealed to you.

If no sign is revealed, you can then perform the 7-card reading again in this manner and divine another day.

This method may also be used as a short-timing method where you wish to divine the day of the week for a matter.

Bonus Method 2: Pooh Sticks Method

A Method for using Rune-staves and Tarot with a little bit of whimsy.

And he went back for some more fir-cones. It did. It kept on doing it. Then he dropped two in at once, and leant over the bridge to see which of them would come out first; and one of them did; but as they were both the same size, he didn't know if it was the one which he wanted to win, or the other one. So the next time he dropped one big one and one little one, and the big one came out first, which was what he had said it would do, and the little one came out last, which was what he had said it would do, so he had won twice ... and then he went home for tea.

And that was the beginning of the game called Poohsticks, which Pooh invented, and which he and his friends used to play on the edge of the Forest. But they played with sticks instead of fir-cones, because they were easier to mark.

A. A. Milne, *The House at Pooh Corner.*

You will need for this divination seven sticks, a Tarot deck, a means of making notches in wood, a bridge, seven small pots of waterproof paint of differing colors, a notepad, and a slowly moving river.

In answer to the question "What is Which and Which is What?" shuffle and select 21 Tarot cards. Note each of these cards and then gather together 7 sticks, preferably Willow. They should be about 4-6 inches long and thicker than a pencil.

Take the 21 cards (remaining face-down) and divide them into 7 stacks of 3. Number the stacks 1-7.

Etch onto the sticks a number of notches starting with one notch on one stick, to seven notches on the seventh stick. Paint onto each a different and bright color and make a note of the colors to the numbers (i.e. red stick = 3 notches).

On a Monday (and this must be a Monday) go to a bridge where you can easily drop (and not throw) the seven sticks from the side of the bridge where the river is flowing down. Then race to the other side of the bridge and with some excitement exclaim the color of the winning stick – the stick emerging first from under the bridge.

You can then consult your notebook to discern the number of notches on that stick, and on returning home, consult the pile of 3 cards bearing that number. To what does the Tarot River answer to "What is Which and Which is What?"

You may also use this method for the other seven questions posed by Pooh, although Tigger did interrupt him before he could complete the seventh. There is one for every day of the week (other than Sunday):

On Monday, when the sun is hot

I wonder to myself a lot:

"Now is it true, or is it not,

"That what is which and which is what?"

Master Method: The Grand Quadrangle

A Master method of using the Runes, I-Ching, the Sabian Symbols and Tarot.

There are a range of oracular devices ranging from the Runes to the I-Ching, Tarot to Astrology. They each have their cultural and philosophical underpinnings. I tend to see the Tarot as a snapshot, the Runes as a narrative, the I-Ching as a flow and Astrology as a blueprint.

Sometimes we have a question that demands due consideration from all angles, and for this occasion we have used the Grand Quadrangle spread. This incorporates Astrology by using the Sabian Symbols – an elegant and enigmatic system of channeled symbols for the Astrological Decans.

In this method, we triangulate and calibrate the various systems like an *Alethiometer* from the works of Phillip Pullman.

Firstly, we cast a Sabian Symbol, from the *Astrological Oracle* App or book which gives various methods to produce a symbol, including the use of dice or by drawing one from the book via Bibliomancy.

This gives us our Grand Title for the Quadrangle and is the outside **format** for the whole reading. We will see how this works in our example following.

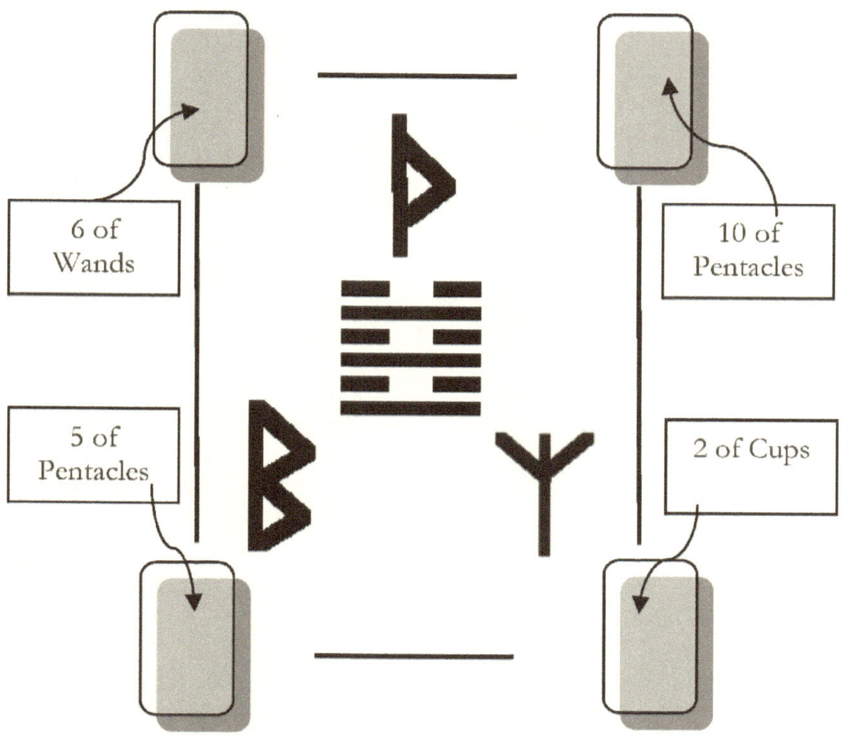

Illus. The Grand Quadrangle.

We then cast an I-Ching Hexagram. This provides the changeable and variable **flow** of the matter within the very center of the frame. This tells us what is already passing and changing.

We then draw 4 Tarot cards which provide the **framework**, giving the general bearing of the situation as a snapshot. This is like a map by which we compare the inner flow and directions of the current (I-Ching) to the destination provided by the grand title of the voyage.

Finally, we draw three Runes to provide the elemental engine or **fuel** for the journey. These provide narrative instructions to the soul to accord life with the direction necessary.

We will now give a worked example of the Grand Quadrangle Method.

Firstly, we cast the Sabian Symbol and receive "Scorpio, 27 degrees", which is defined by "A Military Band on the March". This gives the overall format of the reading as mobilizing towards some specific outcome. It certainly means our reading will call for decisive action!

We then cast our I-Ching Hexgram (using Yarrow Sticks or Coins) and receive I-Ching Hexagram 63. This is *Ji Ji*, "Already Crossing", and signifies Clarity in Action. We can further contemplate this Hexagram and look to the lines which show how the grand title is playing out. In this case, we see advice to keep moving, not chase after any losses. This is further encouragement and so far, a positive reading!

We then draw our Tarot cards to get a pictorial snapshot of the framework in which we should make our actions. These turn out to be the 6 of Wands, 10 of Pentacles, 5 of Pentacles and 2 of Cups. We can read these as a situation where we are seeing a vision being mainly realized but not yet finished (6 of Wands), financial stability (10 of Pentacles) going hand-in-hand with significant investment (5 of Pentacles) and a partnership bearing good initial results (2 of Cups). Again, whilst warning slightly of a tension between stability and investment (the deferred income of the 5 of Pentacles) the general snapshot is also favorable.

Finally, we look to the three Runes we cast to provide the fuel or divination for the direction and action required. These were cast and produced in this reading; Elhaz, Berkano and Thurisaz. These can be interpreted respectively as awakening (but a danger not to attack, but be circumspect), domestic change (in a peaceful manner) and a directed force (but with a warning to not blindly engage the world, but to do so with knowledge). These runes are all slightly double-edged, but in the main signify we should proceed, but hold back a little and be aware we do not know the full lay of the land.

This caution is also intimated in the I-Ching which warns of the fox getting its tail wet in the water of the passing river.

By using these various oracular devices each in their own context, we can create an overall reading which is elegant, comprehensive and dovetails into a meaningful whole.

Recommended Reading

Lyn Birkbeck, *The Astrological Oracle* (London: Thorsons, 2002).

Conclusion

We trust you will find many months of discovery and play with your decks in this second Tarosophy KickStart Guide. It has been a pleasure to produce it and play with the ideas to provide a fresh new look at Tarot.

It is hoped you will feel inspired to play with your deck as a living and breathing oracle in engagement with the world around you. Our next Kickstart Guide, *Tarot Inspire,* explores how to further use Tarot as a spiritual exploration of the mysteries.

These Guides are a prompt for your own exploration, to discover your own voice in Tarot. We encourage the diversity of divination!

We have also provided in the final section a list of reading materials and website resources to discover more in the very best of Tarot and Tarosophy.

Further Reading

The following titles have been chosen specifically to provide further intermediate reading on subjects connected with *Tarot Twist*. They all deal in their own ways with the interconnected universe, a concept in which all Tarosophy resides.

Dreams

James Hall, *Jungian Dream Interpretation* (Inner City Books, 1983).

Science & Religion

Ervin Laszlo, *The Interconnected Universe* (Singapore: World Scientific, 1999).

Mark I. Wallace, *Finding God in the Singing River* (Minneapolis: Fortress Press, 2005).

Lynne McTaggart, *The Field* (New York: Harper Collins, 2002).

Michael Conforti, *Field, Form and Fate* (New Orleans: Spring Journal, 1999).

Louise B. Young, *The Unfinished Universe* (Oxford: Oxford Press, 1993).

Runes & I-Ching

Edred Thorsson, *At The Well of Wyrd* (York Beach: Weiser, 1988).

Stephen Karcher, *Total I-Ching* (London: Time Warner, 2003).

Oracles Contemporary and Ancient

Lon Milo Duquette, *The Book of Ordinary Oracles* (York Beach: Weiser, 2005).

Sarah Iles Johnston, *Ancient Greek Divination* (Chichester: Wiley-Blackwell, 2008).

Tarot

Katz, M. *Tarosophy*. Keswick: Forge Press, 2016.

Katz, M. & Goodwin, T. *Around the Tarot in 78 Days*. Woodbury: Llewellyn, 2012.

Katz, M. & Goodwin, T. *Tarot Flip*. Forge Press, 2012.

The Tyldwick Tarot

The **Tyldwick Tarot,** by Neil Lovell, whose images grace the covers of this Tarosophy Kickstart series, can be viewed online on the comprehensive and beautifully designed site:

http://www.malpertuis.co.uk/tyldwick.

The theme of the deck is that of an elegant house, through which one can wander without "being distracted by a cast of characters" as might be found in other Tarot decks. The cards are beautifully layered and suffused with tonal casts from the international travel that the designer has enjoyed – and not so enjoyed - as described in some fascinating cases which are revealed in the extensive interview on the site.

The deck reminds us very much of the film, *Last Year in Marienbad* (1961, dir. Alain Resnais) which is a dream-like excursion into an environment which may or may not be real, in which the characters not so much inhabit the place, but are extensions of the place itself. In the Tyldwick Tarot, the few characters we see are the Court Cards where faces are reflected in mirrors – or perhaps are even looking out from the other side of the mirrors themselves.

We highly recommend this deck!

Another suitable use for this deck would be as an adjunct to the Inner Guide Meditation work. You can discover more about the ***Inner Guide Meditation*** in the book of the same name by Edwin Steinbrecher (pub. York Beach: Weiser, 1988).

Kindle Tarot Books & Series

Check out all our other books and series for original and exciting ways in which you can use a deck of tarot cards to change your life.

Gated Spreads Series

Set 1

Book 1: *The Tarot Shaman (Contact Your Animal Spirit)*

Book 2: *Gates of Valentine (Love & Relationships)*

Book 3: *The Resurrection Engine (Change Your Life)*

Set 2

Book 4: *Palace of the Phoenix (Alchemy)*

Book 5: *Garden of Creation (Creativity & Inspiration)*

Book 6: *Ghost Train (Explore Your Past)*

Set 3

Coming Soon – Enter the Temple of the Gods.

Tarosophy KickStart Series

Volume I.

Book I: *Tarot Flip* - Reading Tarot Straight from the Box.
Book II: *Tarot Twist* - Finding a Spread for Every Question.
Book III: *Tarot Inspire* – Explore your Spiritual Life with Tarot.

Volume II.

Book I: *Tarot Switch* – Use Magical Tarot methods to change your Life.
Book II: *Tarot Uplift* – Experience Tarot and Kabbalah for Initiation.
Book III: *Tarot Divine* - Encounter the Mystical Teachings of Tarot.

Tarot Life Series

Tarot Life: A revolutionary method to change your life in 12 Kindle pamphlets.

1. Discover Your Destiny

2. Remove The Blocks

3. Make Decisions Better

4. Enter the Flow

5. Ride the Lion

6. Connect to Service

7. Find Equality

8. Die To Your Self

9. Entering Unity

10. Becoming the Real

11. Your Keys to Freedom

12. The Depth of Divinity

Websites & Resources

Tarot Association: http://www.tarotassociation.net

Tarot Professionals Facebook Group

http://www.facebook.com/groups/tarotprofessionals

Free Tarot Card Meanings & Spreads

http://www.mytarotcardmeanings.com